T0284842

The Six Disciplines of Strategic Thinking

The Six Disciplines of Strategic Thinking

Leading Your Organization into the Future

Michael D. Watkins

HARPER
BUSINESS
An Imprint of HarperCollins*Publishers*

HarperCollins books may be purchased for educational, business,
or sales promotional use. For information, please email the Special
Markets Department at SPsales@harpercollins.com.

Originally published in the United Kingdom in 2024 by Ebury Edge,
an imprint of Ebury Publishing.

Illustrations by Matt Lloyd

FIRST U.S. EDITION

Library of Congress Cataloging-in-Publication Data has been applied
for.

ISBN 978-0-06-335796-9

24 25 26 27 28 LBC 8 7 6 5 4

To Katia, love of my life.

CONTENTS

Foreword   ix

Introduction: The Power of Strategic Thinking   1

1. The Discipline of Pattern Recognition   19

2. The Discipline of Systems Analysis   37

3. The Discipline of Mental Agility   63

4. The Discipline of Structured Problem-solving   81

5. The Discipline of Visioning   105

6. The Discipline of Political Savvy   123

Conclusion: Developing Your Strategic-thinking Ability   147

Notes   159

Acknowledgements   167

Index   171

FOREWORD

STRATEGIC THINKING HAS long been essential for leaders in business, government and other organizations. The ability
to anticipate and plan for the future, to think critically and creatively about complex problems and to make effective decisions
in the face of uncertainty and change is vital in today's rapidly
evolving global environment.

Recent developments in technology, globalization, and political and economic instability have only heightened the need for
strategic thinking. The rapid pace of technological change has disrupted traditional business models and created new opportunities
for those who can think strategically about how to leverage them.
The world has become interconnected and interdependent,
requiring leaders to think more broadly and globally about their
operations and markets. And political and economic instability
have created a more uncertain and volatile environment, making it
increasingly difficult for leaders to predict and plan for the future.

In this context, strategic thinking is becoming more important than ever. Leaders who can think strategically will be better
positioned to anticipate and respond to these challenges, and to
capitalize on the opportunities they present. This book provides
a comprehensive and practical guide to strategic thinking, offer-
ing a wealth of insights and tools for leaders at all levels.

While the foundations of strategic thinking by leaders will remain essentially the same, the development of artificial intelligence (AI) will revolutionize how business leaders engage in it. With the ability to process large amounts of data, identify patterns and make predictions, AI will help business leaders with new insights and perspectives that were previously unavailable. This will enable them to make more informed and accurate decisions and to anticipate and plan for the future more effectively. The implications for the future of strategic advisory work by consultants are vast.

In the future, combinations of top leaders and AI-enabled strategic support systems will likely look like *symbiotic relationships* where human leaders and AI systems work together to enhance decision-making, problem-solving and strategy development. The AI systems will provide the leaders with real-time data, analysis and insights that they can use to make better decisions and create better strategies. They can analyze large amounts of data, spot patterns and trends, make predictions and help leaders identify and mitigate risks. They will also be able to simulate different scenarios and provide various options and recommendations.

In these symbiotic relationships, leaders will frame the right questions and interpret the insights and recommendations they provide. As has always been the case, leaders will provide context and contribute creativity. Critically, they will have the emotional intelligence and political savvy to adapt and implement the results.

However, as the use of AI becomes more widespread, it is becoming increasingly important for top business leaders to develop new skills in order to leverage these systems. This includes understanding the technology and the data it generates, being able to interpret and analyze the insights it provides, and having the ability to make decisions based on these insights. Additionally, it's important for leaders to understand the ethical and societal implications of the AI systems they are using.

As you read this book, you therefore should keep in mind that the six disciplines of strategic thinking described here will remain essential and perhaps even increase in importance as we move forwards. At the same time, as you progress through the chapters imagine how you will apply the ideas and tools if you are working with an AI system tailored to your company and optimized to work effectively with you.

THE POWER OF STRATEGIC THINKING

WHEN GENE WOODS became CEO of Carolinas Health-Care System (CHS) in 2016, it was a well-regarded non-profit hospital system located principally in North Carolina with an annual revenue of $8 billion and 60,000 employees. An experienced chief executive with a track record of success, Woods inherited a strong organization with good margins, an AA-rated balance sheet, tremendous depth of clinical talent and a long-tenured leadership team. On the face of it, it was a sustainable success scenario, but storm clouds were on the horizon.

Healthcare in the United States was facing seismic shifts. Expenses were rapidly outstripping revenues, even in the most successful healthcare systems. Political turmoil was creating uncertainty about regulatory policy changes, and private equity firms were funding many new competitors determined to disrupt the market. Anticipating the challenges, the CHS board hired Woods to prepare the organization for the future. "I inherited an organization that was very successful under the old rules," said Woods, who was interviewed extensively for this book. "But where others saw success, I saw tremendous vulnerability."

The US healthcare industry was also going through rapid

consolidation, a trend that Woods thought would continue. While not in immediate jeopardy, he believed CHS could not remain viable for long with its current business model. When he took the helm, the organization had management service agreements with other nearby healthcare systems. CHS managed these systems for a fee, but they were very loosely integrated. Woods thought those types of relationships were losing their currency, as they did not promote the sharing of best practice or create economies of scale. He believed CHS's business model had to become significantly more integrated to meet anticipated future challenges.

CHS was at a pivotal juncture. "I foresaw that we would soon have to make hard choices about whether we could afford to maintain those loosely affiliated relationships," Woods said. "Also, although our core enterprise was strong and in a growing market, with the rapid consolidation happening, I could foresee being surrounded within a few years by other big systems eager to compete for our business. We needed to be the ones to drive consolidation in the region. If we weren't the convener, we would be the convened."

That insight catalyzed the development of what Woods called his "next-generation network strategy." This was his vision of a tightly integrated regional network of systems with aligned missions and cultures that would compete with rivals by sharing best practices, leveraging complementary capabilities and getting the benefits of scale.

To lay the groundwork for realizing his vision, Woods built relationships with other healthcare CEOs and community and government leaders across the region. At the same time, he launched a transformation initiative within CHS to develop a new model for partnering – and a more adaptive culture to support it.

"We had historically been known for a top-down, 'we

manage you, so do as we say' approach," said Woods. "I knew that wouldn't take us where we needed to go. Culturally, we needed to evolve to support the new partnering model."

Fast-forward five years to late 2021, CHS (renamed Atrium Health) had grown into a substantial regional healthcare system with operations in North Carolina, South Carolina, Georgia and Virginia. By joining forces with three nearby healthcare systems, Atrium Health increased its annual revenue to $12 billion and added 17,000 employees, bringing the total to 77,000. It was a transformed organization, poised for additional growth, led by a new leadership team and infused with an inclusive, high-performance culture. Joining forces with Wake Forest Baptist Health, a renowned academic medical system, complemented Atrium Health's clinical excellence with world-class research capabilities. The organization was well-placed to be a nationally recognized leader and spearhead the development of new health-care models. Woods was not content to stop there, however.

In May 2022, Woods and Jim Skogsbergh, the CEO of Advocate Aurora Health, a large non-profit system operating in Wisconsin and Illinois, stunned the US healthcare industry by announcing their intention to merge.[1] Approved by the US Federal Trade Commission and state regulatory authorities in late 2022, the combination created Advocate Health, the fifth-largest non-profit healthcare system in the country with 158,000 employees, $27 billion in revenue, 67 hospitals and more than 1,000 locations offering clinical services. Woods and Skogsbergh would become co-CEOs of the new entity, with Skogsbergh announcing his intention to retire after 18 months, at which point Woods would become sole CEO.

As the principal architect of this remarkable journey from a modest-sized local healthcare system to a national powerhouse,

Woods exemplifies the power of strategic thinking. If you aspire to lead businesses, you must, like Woods, be a strategic thinker. You can go far in organizations by being a solid operator, but you will never succeed at the top without strategic thinking. Why? Because businesses that aren't led by strategic thinkers get outmanoeuvred by those that are – either they are acquired, or they wither and die. Boards select people with strong strategic-thinking capabilities to chart the courses for their businesses through waters littered with rocks and shoals. Every business today is navigating through such challenges.

In 2013, the Management Research Group surveyed 60,000 managers and executives in 140 countries across 26 industries. The results revealed that respondents with superior strategic-thinking skills (defined as critical analysis, thinking ahead and planning) were six times more likely to be seen by colleagues as effective leaders. They were also four times more likely to be perceived as having strong growth potential within their organizations.[2] More recent research by the professional services firm Zenger Folkman, publicized in 2021 but from a few years earlier, supports this assessment. In three separate studies, Zenger Folkman found strong correlations between having a "strategic perspective" and being promoted to senior levels.[3]

The bottom line: strategic thinking is the fast lane to the top. If you don't believe you're a strong enough strategic thinker today, the good news is you can learn to become one. Leaders like Woods unquestionably have natural talent. But they have also worked hard to develop their capacity to lead organizations into the future. In this book, I will show you how. I will help you assess your innate ability to think strategically – and learn to amplify it through experiences and training.

What is strategic thinking?

There have been many efforts to define "strategic thinking," but a good description has remained elusive. When I asked more than 50 senior executives, HR leaders and learning and development professionals to define it, their initial responses boiled down to: "I know it when I see it." They recognized that strategic thinking was a distinct and vital capability in senior leaders; beyond that, things got fuzzy. For some, strategic thinking was the ability to take in a lot of information and figure out what is and isn't important. For others, it was being good at thinking through moves and countermoves. For others still, it was about envisioning the future. There were common themes, to be sure, but no comprehensive definition.

The absence of a good definition makes assessing and developing strategic-thinking ability very difficult. We can only design promising approaches for evaluating and strengthening strategic thinking by isolating the specific building blocks of this skill.

The good news is that when I probed deeper in interviews with business leaders, common themes emerged. Distilling those insights, I developed this definition:

> Strategic thinking is the set of mental disciplines leaders use to recognize potential threats and opportunities, establish priorities to focus attention, and mobilize themselves and their organizations to envision and enact promising paths forward.

In a nutshell: it means looking beyond the present situation and thinking critically and creatively about the many potential futures. Based on your assessment of each imagined scenario's potential risks and opportunities, you can develop promising strategies to move your organization forwards.

The path to being recognized as a strategic thinker requires more than ability; it requires *opportunity*. You could have outstanding strategic-thinking potential but never get recognition if your role hasn't given you a chance to shine. Many senior positions in organizations don't require much strategic thinking; it's enough to have strong analytical, problem-solving and execution capabilities. Securing a role that allows you to demonstrate your strategic-thinking skills is often intensely political. Strategists tend to be quite good at getting opportunities to be strategic. However, the stakes are too high to have the identification and development of strategic thinkers be so dependent on chance and politics.

Reflection: Throughout the book, you will encounter prompts like this. They are invitations to pause your reading and consider the critical questions. As you read my definition of strategic thinking, how does it relate to your abilities, and how could you develop them further?

Strategic thinking versus critical thinking

Critical thinking is a necessary component and foundational skill for strategic thinking, but it's not sufficient on its own. Critical thinking is the ability to evaluate information and arguments logically and systematically. It involves gathering and assessing facts, recognizing assumptions and biases, and evaluating the strengths and weaknesses of arguments. As I will discuss in the rest of the book, strategic thinking also involves anticipation, creativity, vision, goal setting and execution. In addition to thinking critically, strategic thinkers can anticipate and plan for the future, think creatively about complex problems and make effective decisions in the face of uncertainty and change.

Strategic thinking versus creative thinking

Creative thinking is the ability to generate new and innovative ideas. It involves thinking outside the box, questioning assumptions and challenging the status quo. Creative thinking is another important element of strategic thinking because it allows leaders to generate new ideas and perspectives that inform their strategic decisions. In today's rapidly changing business environment, thinking creatively is becoming increasingly important for leaders to stay ahead of the curve. In *Creative Confidence: Unleashing the Creative Potential Within Us All*, Tom and David Kelley show how anyone can learn to be more creative, and they provide concrete ways to do so.[4] By developing the ability to think creatively, as part of a broader effort to develop your strategic-thinking ability, you can better anticipate future trends and develop creative ways to capitalize on them.

Strategic thinking versus design thinking

Strategic thinking and design thinking are both approaches to problem-solving, but they differ in important ways. Strategic thinking involves analyzing an organization's current state and environment, identifying challenges and opportunities, and developing a plan of action to achieve its goals. In contrast, design thinking is a creative process of understanding customers' needs and developing solutions to meet those needs. As summarized in *Design Thinking: Understanding How Designers Think and Work* by Nigel Cross, it involves empathizing with end users, defining problems, generating ideas, prototyping solutions and testing those solutions to see if they work.[5] While strategic thinking is focused on achieving long-term organizational goals and making effective decisions, design thinking is focused on creating innovative solutions to delight customers.

Strategic thinking and contextual awareness

Finally, to be a strong strategic thinker, you must deeply understand the context in which you operate. This means you must have in-depth insight into your organization's internal environment, such as its culture, structure and resources. That insight will allow you to assess your organization's strengths and weaknesses and develop strategies that align with its capabilities. You must also understand the external environment, including the economic, political, social and technological factors impacting on your organization. This will help you anticipate and plan for the changes around you and identify new growth opportunities.

In addition, you must have insight into the expectations and needs of a diverse range of stakeholders, such as customers, shareholders, employees and regulators. This knowledge allows you to anticipate and plan for the needs of these stakeholders and develop strategies that align with their expectations.

Understanding your business context allows you to anticipate and plan for the future more effectively, identify opportunities for growth, and develop strategies that are well-suited to the specific context in which your organization operates. The implication is that you must invest in absorbing and synthesizing information about your organization and the broader external environment in which it operates.

Why is strategic thinking so valuable?

Strategic thinking wouldn't be necessary if the business world were benign, stable and predictable. But, of course, it's none of those things. It's ever more competitive, and the stakes are high. Determining the right strategies to create or sustain success is challenging, and leaders must pilot their organizations through increasingly turbulent waters. The combination of high stakes and challenging environments is what makes strategic thinking so valuable.

To appreciate this, it helps to understand the nature of the mental processing challenges that leaders like Gene Woods at Atrium Health face. Specifically, they confront four dimensions of difficulty: volatility, uncertainty, complexity and ambiguity (VUCA, a term that dates back to the work of Warren G. Bennis and Burt Nanus in the mid-1980s and was subsequently adopted by the US Army and then more broadly in work on leadership).[6]

While VUCA sounds good and is easy to remember, I think the order of the words should be flipped, with complexity at the front (making the acronym CUVA). Complexity, uncertainty, volatility and ambiguity are interrelated, and building on one dimension helps in understanding and addressing the others. Complexity is at the core of the challenges most leaders face. By understanding the complexity of your organization and business environment, you can anticipate and make sense of key uncertainties, which will help you respond to volatility and deal with ambiguity.

- *Complexity* means that the domain of interest (for example, developing new products) has many interconnected variables that make it challenging to comprehend with the limited cognitive capacities that we all have as human beings. An organization with tens of thousands of employees delivering healthcare to thousands of patients daily in hundreds of facilities using many technologies and dozens of processes has an inherently high level of complexity. Complexity makes it challenging for leaders to build and maintain good "mental models" of their organizations and make sound predictions about what will happen if something changes. *Strategic thinkers are skilled at navigating complexity because they understand how systems work and focus their attention on what really matters.*

- *Uncertainty* means dealing with situations with a clear set of potential outcomes but where the specific event that will occur cannot be perfectly predicted. This is the case regardless of how much effort you invest in gathering more information. Often, this is because a host of small contributing factors can influence the outcome. In the case of healthcare in the US, government regulations, which powerfully shape the industry, can evolve very differently depending on the results of national and state elections. *Strategic thinkers isolate the most important uncertainties, think about probabilities and explore the implications of plausible scenarios.*

- *Volatility* means that important things – for example, the price of oil – change rapidly. This makes it challenging to track what is happening and adapt to the changes. In the healthcare example, new competitors focused on the most profitable businesses may spring from nowhere, rendering existing business models obsolete. The intensive pace of technological innovation challenges us to know when and how to adapt. *Strategic thinkers rapidly sense and respond to emerging threats and opportunities.*

■ *Ambiguity* means there are diverse viewpoints about what problems the organization should focus on. There may also be competing perspectives about the potential of different solutions. As a result, stakeholders have divergent views about what is "right." For example, hospital systems in the US face significant pressure to reduce costs, improve financial viability and make care more affordable. Seen from the patient perspective, more affordable care is good. From the standpoint of hospital administrators, who are expected to do more with less, it could force tough trade-offs. *Strategic thinkers negotiate among differing interests and perspectives to create shared "frames" of problems and agreements.*

Today, the CUVA environment impacts every business, making it challenging for leaders to chart the right paths forward. The intensity of these challenges is also increasing due to technological, social and environmental changes. The implication is that the value of strategic thinking is, therefore, growing.

Reflection: To what extent are you and your organization facing challenges due to complexity, uncertainty, volatility and ambiguity? Which of the CUVA dimensions are creating the greatest challenges?

What strategic thinking is not

A good working definition of strategic thinking also helps us clarify what strategic thinking is not. There is a tendency to focus on the strategic part, not the thinking part.

It's not competitive analysis. That's taking a framework for analyzing competitors in your industry – for example, Michael Porter's

Five Forces[7] – and applying it to your organization's context to gain insight into what's important and what to do. *Competitive analysis is often an essential input into strategic thinking.*

It's not strategic planning. That's the process organizations use to define their strategies, including making choices about what to do and not to do, allocating resources to supporting activities, and creating criteria for making decisions consistent with the strategy. *Strategic planning can be powerfully informed and shaped by strategic thinking.*

While competitive analysis and strategic planning are valuable activities (and there are many books, articles and programmes about them), strategic thinking is different. Competitive analysis and planning are deductive and analytical; strategic thinking is more inductive and more about synthesis. Also, where competitive analysis and strategic planning are typically collective organizational processes, strategic thinking relies more on the individual leader engaging in the correct modes of mental processing that result in actionable insights and promising strategies.

Are great strategic thinkers born or made?

As with most exceptional human capabilities, the answer is "both." An element of inborn ability – your *endowment* – will likely limit your potential to be a strategic thinker. However, as mentioned above, effective strategic thinking is more than raw analytical ability. Emotional intelligence, creativity and the ability to collaborate and communicate effectively also play a crucial role. Business leaders who understand and manage their own emotions and those of others, think creatively and generate new ideas, and communicate and work effectively with others are likely to be more effective strategic thinkers.

Regardless of your endowment, the right experiences and training can help you develop that potential. It's like deciding to become a marathon runner. Your genetics – having a higher percentage of slow-twitch muscle fibres and greater lung capacity – may make it easier to become a strong marathon runner.[8] But if you don't run – *a lot* – and discipline yourself to practise using the proper techniques, you will likely lose out to people with less inherent potential but greater discipline.

Perhaps you are among the fortunate few born to be strategic thinkers. You emerged into the world with the natural analytical ability, emotional intelligence and creative potential needed to become a brilliant leader of businesses. Most likely, however, this is not the case. Take heart, because strategic thinking is an ability you can develop. While inherent ability helps, everyone can learn to do it better. It just takes knowing how to develop yourself and a disciplined commitment to doing the work.

The following equation defines your strategic-thinking capacity (STC):

STC = Endowment + Experience + Exercise

Your *endowment* is your natural ability that stems from your genetics and upbringing. *Experience* comes from your engagement in situations that develop your strategic-thinking ability. *Exercise* is the mental work you do to build your strategic-thinking muscles.

Many leaders struggle with the *experience* part of the equation because they don't get opportunities to demonstrate and develop their potential. This means you must actively seek out new challenges and responsibilities. This can include taking on new projects, leading cross-functional teams and exploring opportunities for new roles that require more strategic thinking. By taking on new challenges, you will be exposed to new and diverse experiences, which can help to broaden your perspective and develop your strategic-thinking abilities.

Regarding the *exercise* element, I offer suggestions about strengthening your strategic-thinking ability throughout the book and summarize this advice at the end.

What is the role of personality?

Strategic thinking is rooted in cognitive and emotional capacities, but personality also plays a role. Specifically, there are three essential personality prerequisites for being a strong strategic thinker. The first is openness to new experiences. Great strategic thinkers adapt to changing circumstances and integrate new information into their assessments. The second is an unshakeable confidence that you can anticipate and proactively shape the future for yourself and your organization and not just react to emerging developments. The third is a drive to win. Ambition is a necessary quality in great strategic thinkers.

The six disciplines of strategic thinking

This book is founded on my belief, supported by research and practical experience, that you can develop your strategic-thinking ability. If you get the right exposure and do the right exercises, you will substantially increase your ability to think strategically. This will help you get to the top and lead your organization into the future.

In the following chapters, I will explore six mental disciplines that constitute strategic thinking. These disciplines allow you to recognize emerging challenges and opportunities, prioritize what really matters and mobilize your organization to respond proactively.

The first three disciplines are the foundation of your ability to *recognize and prioritize* the challenges and opportunities facing your organization:

> *Discipline 1: Pattern recognition* – Your ability to observe complex, uncertain, volatile and ambiguous (CUVA) business scenarios, rapidly figure out what is and isn't essential, and identify critical threats and opportunities.
>
> *Discipline 2: Systems analysis* – Your ability to mentally model complex situations as systems and leverage those models to recognize patterns, make predictions and develop promising strategies.
>
> *Discipline 3: Mental agility* – Your ability to explore business challenges using different levels of analysis, and anticipate the actions and reactions of other stakeholders as they pursue their own goals.

The other three disciplines enhance your ability to *mobilize* your organization to deal with challenges and opportunities effectively:

> *Discipline 4: Structured problem-solving* – Your ability to direct your organization to frame problems, develop creative solutions and make tough choices in the most effective ways.
>
> *Discipline 5: Visioning* – Your ability to imagine potential futures that are ambitious and achievable and energize your organization to realize them.

Discipline 6: Political savvy – Your understanding of how influence works in organizations and ability to leverage those insights to build alliances with key stakeholders.

For each of the six disciplines, I explore what they are and how you can develop them. At the end of the book, I distil this advice in an "exercise programme" for becoming a stronger strategic thinker.

AI and the future of strategic thinking

Finally, developments in artificial intelligence (AI) will continue to augment and amplify human strategic-thinking ability. Machine learning systems trained on vast bases of general and specialized business knowledge and accessed through conversational natural language interfaces are revolutionizing how leaders engage in the strategic-thinking process. With the ability to process large amounts of data, identify patterns and make predictions, AI helps leaders gain new insights and perspectives that were previously unavailable.

Increasingly, leaders are forming symbiotic relationships with AI-enabled strategic systems to enhance decision-making, problem-solving and strategy development. These systems provide real-time data, analysis and insights, as well as simulating different scenarios and providing various options and recommendations.

Fortunately, at least for now, the six disciplines of strategic thinking remain important capabilities for business leaders (like you!) to develop. In these symbiotic human–AI relationships, leaders will continue to apply the six disciplines to ask the right questions and interpret the insights and recommendations your AI partners provide. Critically, you will provide context, contribute creativity and apply emotional intelligence and political savvy to adapt and implement the results.

To learn more

Creative Confidence: Unleashing the Creative Potential Within Us All by Tom and David Kelley

Design Thinking: Understanding How Designers Think and Work by Nigel Cross

Chapter 1

THE DISCIPLINE OF PATTERN RECOGNITION

PATTERN RECOGNITION IS the ability of the human brain to identify and detect regularities or patterns in the world around us. It is a fundamental aspect of human cognition, allowing us to "make sense" of the vast amount of information that constantly bombards us. Human pattern recognition is a complex, dynamic process that involves many different cognitive functions, such as perception, attention, memory and reasoning. It allows us to recognize familiar objects and scenes, make predictions and inferences about the world and learn from experience.

In business, pattern recognition is your ability to observe the CUVA domains in which your organization operates and identify what's important. Strategic thinkers possess powerful mental models of cause-and-effect relationships in their domains of expertise, such as customer behaviour, financial trends and market conditions.

By developing your pattern-recognition abilities, you will better perceive emerging business challenges and opportunities. As a result, you will move more rapidly to prioritize and mobilize your organization to avoid value destruction by neutralizing threats, or creating value by capitalizing on opportunities, or some combination of those two outcomes.

As shown in Figure 1, below, strategic thinking is the process through which you recognize, prioritize and mobilize (RPM) to deal with challenges and opportunities. This is a cyclical process in which recognition of problems leads to prioritizing the most important ones and then mobilizing your organization to solve those problems. Moving rapidly through RPM cycles has great value because it will help you – and your team – move faster than competitors.

As illustrated in the Introduction, Gene Woods has outstanding RPM capabilities. When he was named CEO of Carolinas HealthCare System (CHS) in 2016, he foresaw a

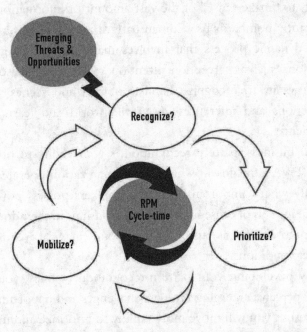

Figure 1: The recognize–prioritize–mobilize cycle

dramatic increase in merger and acquisition activity in US healthcare, driven by declining profits, uncertainty over regulatory policy, and new market entrants funded with private capital. Seeing these emerging patterns, Woods concluded that the industry was ripe for consolidation.

He soon realized that many of his fellow CEOs recognized the potential but had no takeover targets or plans. "Many were heads-down, dealing with significant market dynamics," Woods says. "This became a heads-up conversation, and that created new possibilities." Woods rapidly identified opportunities, then charted a promising path forward for his organization. In 2018, CHS merged with the Georgia-based healthcare system Navicent Health, and the combined entity was renamed Atrium Health. The enlarged company subsequently completed several acquisitions and, in 2022, combined with another large organization, as mentioned in the Introduction, to form the fifth largest non-profit healthcare system in the United States.

Why is pattern recognition so valuable?

If you can't recognize threats and opportunities, you cannot prioritize and mobilize your organization to deal with them. Like most executives, you likely are steering your business through rapid changes in competition, technology and society. At the same time, you are under ever more pressure to improve performance and transform your organization. In such challenging times, you face increasing mental-processing challenges. You must be able to assess rapidly evolving situations, predict their trajectories and adapt your strategies accordingly.

That is where pattern recognition comes in so handy. Insight is power. If you can better recognize patterns in complex, fast-changing environments, you can act more rapidly and effectively than your competitors.

Reflection: To what extent is pattern recognition important in your day-to-day work? What types of patterns are most consequential, and how effective do you believe you are in recognizing them?

Games of strategy, such as chess and Go, are classic domains in which pattern recognition is essential to success. What makes chess grandmasters so much better than average players? One key is their superior ability to perceive important patterns on the chess board and understand the implications for their future moves. In *Improve Your Chess Pattern Recognition*, Arthur van de Oudeweetering notes, "Pattern recognition is one of the most important mechanisms of chess improvement. Realizing that the position on the board is similar to ones you have seen before helps you quickly grasp the essence of that position and find the most promising continuation."[1]

The evolution of computer programs developed to play strategy games further highlights the power of pattern recognition. In 1997, IBM's Deep Blue became the first computer system to win a chess match against reigning world champion Garry Kasparov. Deep Blue's strength came from applying brute-force computing power, using a high-speed machine to search for all potential combinations of moves and countermoves. The engine could evaluate 200 million positions per second and typically searched to a depth of between 6 and 8 moves out, to a maximum of 20 moves or even more in some situations.

Today's best chess engines use a combination of brute-force calculation and deep-learning algorithms running on neural networks.[2] These types of systems are increasingly better than people in even more challenging strategy games. In 2017, AlphaGo, a deep-learning system designed by Google's DeepMind unit, decisively defeated Ke Jie, the world's top-ranked Go professional.[3]

The good news, at least for now, is that emerging AI systems augment and amplify business leaders' pattern-recognition abilities – and the other disciplines of strategic thinking – and don't replace them. That's because the domains in which you operate are not just complex and uncertain, they are also volatile and ambiguous. To be an effective part of a symbiotic human– AI system, you will still need the ability to discern important patterns amid a sea of noise and leverage those insights to frame the most important problems, ask the right questions, prioritize action and mobilize your organization. Your creativity and vision too will remain important in an era when competition intensifies, technological progress accelerates, and political and environmental crises are business as usual.

How does pattern recognition work?

Executives who are good at pattern recognition match their observations about what is happening in the world to their memory patterns. That helps them to rapidly identify what is important to focus on. Strategic thinkers leverage their mental models to "make sense" of what is going on and translate insight into action.

At its best, pattern recognition involves going beyond perceiving the events around us. It's about understanding their broader significance and anticipating how the already dynamic business landscape will likely evolve. Jack Welch, the late former CEO of General Electric (GE) and one of America's most influential business leaders, noted: "Seeing around corners is what differentiates the good leader. Not many people have that. Not many people can predict that corner."[4]

Strong strategic thinkers process vast quantities of information to make rapid, effective judgements about what's essential in the complex business landscape. The mental models they have developed in long-term memory also allow them to perceive weak but important signals in a sea of noise. As a result, they can make decisions based on incomplete information, and in the face of great uncertainty.

To be a great strategic thinker, you must therefore strive to develop powerful mental models of what is happening in the most critical domains of your business. Doing so will help you process more information without stretching your cognitive processing capacity so thinly that you lose focus or get confused. Research shows that information overload saps our energy and self-control, impairs decision-making ability and makes us less collaborative.[5]

To develop your pattern-recognition abilities, it helps to understand that your brain has two basic "systems" of thinking, as described by Nobel laureate Daniel Kahneman in a *Scientific American* excerpt of his book *Thinking, Fast and Slow*:

> The capabilities of System 1 include innate skills that we share with other animals. We are born prepared to perceive the world around us, recognize objects, orient attention, avoid losses, and fear spiders. Other mental activities become fast and automatic through prolonged practice.[6]

System 1 operates in the background, quickly and naturally, with little conscious thought. But it's prone to bias and error. System 2 is more deliberate, slower and more analytical. As Kahneman describes it in the same excerpt, "System 2 allocates attention to the effortful mental activities that demand it, including complex computations. The operations of System 2 are often associated with the subjective experience of agency, choice, and concentration." This second system gets called to action when you are focusing on challenging cognitive tasks, such as mathematics. It "takes control" of your attention when it spots patterns, such as being surprised by new stimuli.

To illustrate, imagine you are a financial services CEO who has set aside provisions for loan losses to hedge against what you believe will be an impending recession. However, your quarterly results beat consensus earnings estimates. As you digest the data, your System 2 taps into your long-term memory, seeking similar patterns you have previously experienced. (It could be government stimulus or a rise in employment, lowering defaults among borrowers.) You then begin constructing a narrative to help you remember, understand, and communicate what you are "seeing."

Leveraging these insights, you shift to envisioning the future through what is known as "associative activation." The processing of one thought (say, government stimulus) sparks the immediate activation of related ideas stored in your long-term memory (say, quantitative easing, liquidity, inflation). This leads to "priming", a phenomenon whereby exposure to one stimulus makes you react faster to related stimuli by speeding up your cognitive processing and memory retrieval. Priming is like ripples in water. Many associations can be formed that, in turn, "prime" other ideas.

How does this sort of mental priming work in business leadership? Imagine you are leading a company that is performing poorly, with falling sales and profits and a decreasing share price.

When you see these poor results, memories of activist investors who believe they can fix the firm's problems may spring to mind. Because your brain is primed to think of this information, you can think fast and react rapidly when you see a potential challenge develop (such as a hedge fund buying a larger stake in the company and pushing for a seat on the board). In essence, you can better sense and respond to emerging threats and opportunities, which is the bedrock of strategic thinking.

These pattern-recognition processes are essential to decision-making and strategy development. Pattern recognition allows you to identify trends, relationships and other meaningful information from a large amount of data. You can then leverage these insights, make more informed decisions, develop more effective strategies and anticipate future events. Additionally, recognizing patterns in data can also help you to identify potential risks and opportunities, which is critical for effective strategy development.

It's likely that you don't even realize it's happening because your brain is primarily controlled by System 1, which moves rapidly and automatically. So, you must focus on developing your brain's System 2 capabilities as part of your wider exercise programme for strengthening your strategic-thinking ability.

Reflection: How can you become more aware of when you are, and are not, engaged in Kahneman's System 2 thinking?

What are the limitations of pattern-recognition ability?

As you develop your pattern-recognition abilities, it's also essential to understand the limitations and avoid falling into some common traps. Failing to recognize fundamental cognitive limitations is one such pitfall. You cannot hope to sense and respond to every significant development impacting on your business. We all have a limited capacity for attention and focusing too intensely on one task can render you blind, in essence, to things that would typically draw your gaze.

A classic illustration of this is "The Invisible Gorilla," an experiment run by Christopher Chabris and Daniel Simons. They asked students on a psychology course at Harvard University to watch a video and count how many times the players passed a basketball. More than half the participants were completely oblivious to a person walking through the game in a gorilla suit, pounding their chest. Even after the students were told about the gorilla, with the benefit of hindsight, they could not recall it.[7] Their minds focused on the activity they were told was critical, leaving little spare capacity to spot even a very novel stimulus.

It's a legacy of evolutionary biology that we prioritize the gravest threats and most promising opportunities to boost our chances of survival. In business, focus enables leaders to concentrate on critical tasks without becoming overwhelmed by an abundance of stimuli. But it comes packaged with potential downsides, especially as the world becomes more complicated and confusing.

The implication, paradoxically, is to be wary about the pitfalls of selective attention. If you can take some time to assess and reflect, you'll be better able to detect the patterns that matter and not get distracted by shiny objects. Like most executives, you probably face increasing demands on your time, and ever more complex challenges as technological, social and ecological developments accelerate. But that just underlines the import-ance of enhancing your ability to detect patterns.

Beyond recognizing the dangers of limited and selective attention, it is crucial to understand that we are vulnerable to biases that impede our ability to perceive the most critical threats and opportunities. In *The Black Swan*, Nassim Nicholas Taleb writes that leaders continually fail to see significant yet unlikely threats (think of the 2008 global financial crisis) or opportun-ities (the emergence of cryptocurrencies and blockchain as a transformational technology).[8]

You won't become great at pattern recognition if you're unaware of your biases in collecting and interpreting informa-tion. Kahneman calls the human mind "a machine for jumping to conclusions." The absence of good information leads us to make assumptions. If those assumptions are reasonably good ones, and the costs are not too high if they turn out to be wrong, then this mental shortcut helps us navigate complex events with-out having the complete picture.[9]

It is essential, though, that you strive to avoid classic traps such as *confirmation bias* – the tendency to seek out new data that are consistent with your pre-existing viewpoints, or to recall evidence that confirms your existing theories.

A related bias, called the "narrative trap," is to perceive pat-terns that simply aren't there. We naturally try and "make sense" of complex, seemingly disparate events by constructing stories and ascribing cause and effect. To illustrate, consider the finan-cial news media. Bank stocks are often said to boom "on the back of" an interest-rate rise, but this analysis fails to account for coincidence or may not control for important contributing variables.

Another version of confirmation bias is *the halo effect*, as described in Phil Rosenzweig's book with the same title.[10] This is the tendency for one important aspect of a person (or a company) to shape perceptions of the whole in ways not supported by the facts. In his research on the halo effect, Rosenzweig showed that it powerfully distorts our thinking about company performance. He explains that it's common to assume a company with a robust financial performance has a sound strategy and strong leadership. However, when performance wanes, we're often quick to conclude that its strategy is unsound and that its CEO has become arrogant. Tangible overall results create a general impression (a halo) that informs our perception of the more granular elements contributing to firm performance. Or, as Rosenzweig put it, we confound outputs with inputs.

Wishful thinking – known more formally as the *sunk cost fallacy* – is another important cognitive bias. It leads us to invest precious resources into a losing proposition in the vain hope of recouping previous losses. This tendency to "double down" has been at the heart of many financial scandals, such as when rogue financial traders trap themselves in a downward spiral of increasingly large and risky bets that, in some cases, have contributed to institutional failure and even global crises.

Finally, it's essential to avoid blaming others when things go wrong. It is a natural human tendency to blame outside factors for negative results while also taking personal credit for positive outcomes. Psychologists call this "self-serving bias." And while it may contribute to perceptions of personal success and political power, it can cloud judgement, leading to potentially catastrophic errors. Strategic thinkers avoid the natural urge to scapegoat. Instead, they unearth and reform the structures that drive poor performance. They are curious and open to a wide range of potential solutions to their challenges.

The implication is that you cannot assess your organization's rapidly shifting realities if you have crippling biases in collecting and interpreting information. "Garbage in, garbage out," as the aphorism so aptly puts it. You will not accurately identify potential threats and opportunities and use these insights to envision and enact the right course of action for your company.

Clearly, you must learn to recognize and avoid common cognitive biases. But that's not enough. Beyond "debiasing" yourself, you must also develop critical-thinking skills that focus and test your pattern-recognition abilities. In a novel situation with high stakes, you must be intentional in critiquing your initial perceptions of the situation. Cognitive biases can obscure important realities, causing us to see what we want to see. The best strategic thinkers are sceptical about their intuitions and challenge everyone's convictions.

Leaders like Woods tend to choose paths that advance their plans and goals; however, pattern recognition can also indicate that you need to adjust course to respond to what is happening around you. Continuous adaptation is a hallmark of great strategic thinkers. As in Woods's case, it often starts with an open discussion – the right environment for strategic thinking to flourish. Best practice includes discussing the potential implications with diverse teams, who will offer a variety of viewpoints and experiences that can improve problem-solving and decision-making.

The discussion can, for example, highlight problems with your mental model, such as when new observations contradict your original assessment of the business landscape, rendering a strategic plan unreliable. You can collect more information and revise your assumptions to make better judgements. Through this process of critiquing and correcting, strategic thinkers can test and improve the fruits of pattern recognition.

Reflection: What can you do to avoid falling into these traps, cultivate your curiosity and ensure that you are updating your mental models?

How can you improve your pattern-recognition ability?

While it is essential to watch out for ways in which pattern recognition can let you down, don't let that detract from its enormous power. The capacity to recognize patterns is built into our brains. But, like the other disciplines of strategic thinking, it can also be developed.

Research on neuroplasticity has shown that the brain directs attention and rallies effort to activities that strain our cognitive abilities.[11] As you learn, you become better at your craft, and your mind no longer works as hard. The regions of the brain that govern attention and effortful control show much-reduced activity.

Total immersion is the best way to learn a new language. It's also a great way to gain deep insight into complex business environments. Immersion is essential because people need significant "soak time" in a milieu to build powerful mental models. (Note to talent-development professionals: this insight also highlights the dangers of moving people too rapidly from business to business or job to job, because there isn't time to master the core dynamics of each new situation.)

You cannot hope to develop superior pattern recognition in every business domain. You must immerse yourself deeply in selected areas – for example, business functions such as marketing, industries like fast-moving consumer goods or stakeholder environments such as government relations. The implication: you need to put a lot of thought into selecting the domains in which you aspire to become a strategic thinker. Only then can you get the necessary immersion and training to become great at pattern recognition.

Another way to develop your pattern-recognition ability is to work closely with "experts" in apprenticeship-like relationships. Find opportunities where you can observe and learn from the work of people who are great at pattern recognition and so absorb their ways of thinking. This requires more than observation, as you want to learn as much as possible about the internal thought processes of the expert. Of course, this means they must be willing to devote some time to discussing their thought processes with you. Helpful questions to ask include:

- What were the most important patterns or signals you perceived?
- What connections did you make to previous situations or events you have experienced?
- What, if anything, was novel about the situation or problem?
- How confident are you in your conclusions?
- To what extent will you continue to refine your thinking and adjust your approach?

Additionally, it helps to intentionally cultivate your curiosity and cast a wide net for information sources. Psychologists have found that simply being curious spurs the urge to explore, discover and grow[12] – which is useful when you need to get into the finer details of the microenvironment, which you may otherwise overlook.

Focus too on looking for trends. For example, you could look at news reports and research, or obtain information through networking, and focus on developing hypotheses about those trends.

Leaders like Woods have decades of experience that enable them to see critical patterns, but they also work hard to supplement this knowledge and strengthen their mental models. As Woods says, "You need to be able to absorb a broad spectrum of data points, qualitative dynamics, experiences – and connect the dots – to form a hypothesis about the best bets to make on the future."

Making a similar point in an interview with the American business magazine *Inc.*, Fred W. Smith, the founder, former CEO and now executive chairman of FedEx, summarized his approach to taking in information about what is going on in the world, describing it as:

> The ability to assimilate information from many different disciplines all at once – particularly information about change, because from change comes opportunity. So, you might be reading something about the cultural history of the United States and come to some realization about where the country is headed demographically.

Smith went on to say that he reads close to four hours a day, consuming "everything from newspapers to books on management theory and flight theory. I try to keep up with the latest technological developments through journals. And I'm fascinated with the future."[13]

Case study analysis is another powerful approach that will help you improve your pattern recognition. You can absorb the lessons and build powerful mental models by consuming a diverse range of realistic "cases" (in-depth studies of a group, event, organization or industry) and reflecting on the experiences depicted. Research suggests that exposure to depictions of reality is particularly impactful.[14]

Simulation is another powerful way to enhance your pattern-recognition abilities. By exposing yourself to situations like those you encounter in the real world, for example through participation in business simulations, you can improve your situational awareness, pattern recognition and even strategic planning and execution. Simulations are an excellent way to train those all-important mental processes that enable us to think critically and strategically and make better choices.

Good feedback is also a powerful tool for developing your pattern-recognition abilities. Research shows that when people are given detailed performance feedback after completing a task, they rapidly converge on the optimal trade-off between speed and accuracy in decision-making.[15] That's because feedback provides reference points and reinforces associations between cues and strategies, helping you to develop the mental models that enable rapid decision-making in uncertain environments with incomplete information. Through feedback, executives can also test their convictions and overcome the cognitive limitations and biases that often lead to poor decisions and bad outcomes.

Summary

Pattern recognition is an important aspect of strategic thinking because it enables you to identify patterns and trends in data and information. This allows you to gain a deeper understanding of your operations, markets and customers – and to identify potential challenges and opportunities. If you can't recognize essential patterns in the most important domains in which your business operates, you have no hope of focusing on what matters and developing good strategies. So work on strengthening your pattern-recognition capabilities through immersion, observation and distillation. The next chapter explores how the discipline of *systems analysis* can enhance your pattern-recognition abilities.

Pattern recognition checklist

Lists like this are included at the end of each chapter to summarize the key takeaways and help get you started in developing each dimension of strategic thinking.

1. What are the most important domains in which you need to develop your pattern-recognition abilities?
2. How can you best immerse yourself in those domains to enhance your mental models?
3. What practices can you use to develop your pattern-recognition abilities, such as learning from simulations, working with experts or getting feedback?
4. What can you do to cultivate your curiosity and get more in tune with emerging trends?
5. How should you develop your awareness of your potential vulnerabilities to cognitive biases?
6. What processes can you implement to help debias yourself and strengthen your critical-thinking ability?

To learn more

Thinking, Fast and Slow by Daniel Kahneman

The Halo Effect . . . and the Eight Other Business Delusions that Deceive Managers by Phil Rosenzweig

Naturalistic Decision Making edited by Caroline E. Zsambok and Gary Klein

CHAPTER 2

THE DISCIPLINE OF SYSTEMS ANALYSIS

SYSTEMS ANALYSIS IS about building mental models of complex domains, such as the competitive environment in which your business operates. The process of creating systems models consists of: (1) breaking complex phenomena down into sets of component elements; (2) understanding how those elements interact; and (3) using that information to build good representations of the most important cause–effects relationships in the business world.

Internally, systems analysis enables you to identify the interconnections and dependencies between different parts of your organization, such as functions, processes and systems. By understanding how different parts of the organization interact and influence each other, you can identify opportunities for improvement, and develop strategies to optimize performance.

Externally, you can use systems analysis to understand the environment in which your organization operates. By analyzing how your organization interacts with external forces, such as customers, suppliers, competitors and governments, you can identify opportunities for growth and develop effective strategies to capitalize on them.

What is systems analysis?

Systems analysis is a holistic approach that focuses on the connections and interactions between the elements of a system rather than on the individual components in isolation. Systems analysis is based on the idea that the interactions between the parts determine the behaviour of a system. As a result, changes in one part of the system can have cascading effects on other elements. It is a valuable tool for solving complex problems and for making decisions that consider the potential impacts and implications of different courses of action.

Systems models can enhance your pattern-recognition ability by reducing the cognitive load required to focus on what is most important. As a result, you more quickly "see" emerging challenges and opportunities. This, in turn, allows you to predict likely impacts more rapidly, and develop strategies to change system dynamics in desired ways.

Systems analysis is an essential tool for scientists studying the world's climate, and economists seeking to forecast the dynamics and evolution of the global economy. Here, the phenomena are far too complex to be dealt with as a whole and are beyond human capacity to fully understand. They must be broken down into subsystems that are modelled independently. For climate scientists, this means creating models of the atmosphere, ocean, cryosphere (areas covered by frozen water) and biosphere. These submodels are developed separately (and themselves consist of multiple elements) and can be used alone or coupled together to generate useful predictions for the global climate.[1] In both climate and economic modelling, computer-based system models, powered by analytical and pattern-recognition algorithms, augment and amplify human ability in symbiotic relationships.

Engineers have long used systems models, often supported by computer-based modelling to design complex products. These models capture processes that happen in parallel and sequentially. They are used to maximize throughput and productivity (e.g. by reducing the costs of holding inventory).

Product development professionals, meanwhile, use "architectural" models in their design processes. Hi-tech products are far too complex to design as a single unit. Take, for example, today's increasingly autonomous vehicles. They incorporate a dizzying array of components – sensors, actuators, processors and algorithms, in addition to more traditional elements such as engines, drivetrains and chassis. Autonomous vehicles are designed as systems consisting of many elements that can be worked on independently and then integrated, so long as the agreed interface specifications are honoured.

Reflection: Have you learned about systems analysis in the past? Have you applied it in your work? If so, was it helpful?

Why is systems analysis so valuable?

To be a more effective strategic thinker, you can learn to create systems models that enhance your ability to recognize patterns, make predictions, formulate strategies, make good decisions and take action faster. These may be formal models that run on computers, but often they are mental models that you "run" inside your head.

You can model many relevant business domains as systems: production processes, organizations, industries and economies. For business leaders, it's essential to leverage systems analysis to understand the internal dynamics of your organization and the economic, political and social forces that shape its external environment.

Our minds naturally try to break complicated problems into constituent elements to make complex tasks easier to handle. While it's important to understand those elements in isolation, knowing how they fit together and interact is also essential. If you fail to do so, you're likely to be "predictably surprised" by what occurs.

As an example, consider what happened in March 2021 when the *Ever Given*, a skyscraper-sized container ship, got wedged across the Suez Canal for six days. An unfortunate navigation error rapidly fractured supply chains and disrupted global trade. The blockage stopped international trade valued at over $9 billion daily, equivalent to $400 million worth of trade per hour, or $6.7 million per minute.[2] Even after the Suez Canal was cleared, it took weeks for global trade flows to stabilize.

Why did this happen? Because global trade is a very complex and surprisingly fragile system. The relentless drive for economic efficiency – particularly the desire to minimize the cost of holding inventory – results in materials and components being transported from many locations over great distances to arrive "just in time" for the next production stage.

While things are stable, this system operates smoothly and efficiently. It's brittle, however – highly vulnerable to small failures. Because there is so little slack and redundancy built into the system, those small failures can rapidly cascade to generate more and bigger problems. As Lukas Kinigadner, the CEO and co-founder of mobile data company Anyline puts it, "Our supply chains are the arteries of industry, and in the era of same-day delivery and 'just-in-time' inventory, even a small blockage can cause . . . disruptions down the line."[3]

Analysts of the global logistics system had long predicted that minor disruptions would have significant consequences. While they couldn't specify the initiating event, they knew that international trade was vulnerable to "cascading systems failures," in which one small problem generates a breakdown somewhere else, triggering more problems and potentially leading to collapse.[4] However, few companies had built slack and redundancy into their supply chains; most would not be able to avoid the impact.

While the specific nature, location and timing of the blockage of the Suez Canal were not predictable, the potential for something to disrupt a vital transportation link in the global trade system was recognized. This example highlights how systems analysis supports the creation of contingency plans. While you cannot predict precisely what crisis will strike, you can anticipate broad classes of financial, ecological, social, and political disasters that could impact on your business. These insights provide a robust basis for designing crisis response plans for your business that deal with potential problems.

Consider how the systemic impacts of the COVID-19 pandemic spiralled into a full-blown economic crisis with production meltdowns and a collapse in consumption and confidence. Savvy investors leveraged their understanding of how markets behave under stress to anticipate how COVID-19 would cascade. They rapidly recognized that a minority of companies would prosper during the pandemic. For example, some pharmaceutical companies were boosted by COVID-19 vaccines, technology giants reaped the rewards from the remote-working revolution, and online retailers benefited from lockdowns.

Leveraging these insights, keen investors quickly moved money out of vulnerable sectors like travel and tourism into potential winners. Bill Ackman, for example, who runs the hedge fund Pershing Square Capital Management, bet that insurance premiums would rise in 2020 as COVID-19 caused economies to lock down. On the strength of a $27 million investment, he made a $2.6 billion profit.[5]

Systems analysis is a powerful tool for managing complexity, focusing attention and taking action. The world is neither stable nor predictable; it is ever more dynamic and complex. This creates risk and uncertainty, leading to information overload. Systems analysis helps you to quickly cut through the noise to identify what is and isn't essential. Done well, it enables you to see further around corners – as Jack Welch put it – and it equips you with the insights you'll need to turn potentially damaging disruption to your organization's advantage.

Reflection: What challenges does your organization face for which systems analysis would be a helpful tool?

How does systems analysis work?

System models have three components: elements, interconnections (or "interfaces") and a purpose or function. To illustrate, think of how your organization could be modelled as a system. For your business to succeed, you must integrate diverse functions and talents into a whole that's greater than the sum of its parts. As Katherine Bach Kalin, a former HR executive who now sits on multiple corporate boards, says, "It's essential to make connections among the people, functions and processes, looking at the enterprise and the opportunities more broadly. You must understand how to manage a business holistically and what you need regarding resources across every function."

Efforts to apply systems analysis to organizational design began in the 1970s. Jay Galbraith, then a professor at Wharton School, first published his Star Model of organizational systems in 1978.[6] Then in 1980, the consultancy McKinsey introduced the "7-S Framework." The models are similar. Galbraith divided organizations into five interconnected elements arrayed in the shape of a star: strategy, structure, processes, rewards and people. McKinsey modelled organizational systems as consisting of seven elements: strategy, structure, systems, staff (people), style (culture), skills and shared values (purpose).[7] Of the two models, Galbraith's Star Model better withstood the test of time and is still used by many business leaders, perhaps because the star makes for a more visually appealing diagram, and five elements are easier to remember than seven.

The system model shown in Figure 2, below, is my adaptation

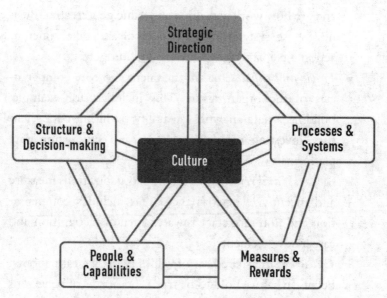

Figure 2: An adaptation of Galbraith's Star Model

of Galbraith's. I broadened "strategy" to "strategic direction" so it encompasses mission, vision, purpose, strategy and key objectives. I also added decision-making, capabilities, systems, and a new element – culture – in the middle.

- *Strategic direction* is your organization's purpose, vision, values, mission, goals and strategy. It aligns people on what needs to be done, how it will be accomplished and why people should get excited about being part of the journey.
- *Structure and decision-making* are about how people are organized in units and groups, how their work is coordinated – e.g. through cross-functional teams – and who has the authority to make decisions.
- *Processes and systems* are flows of materials and information. Processes run laterally through the organization and are how work gets done and value gets created. Businesses use systems to exert control and take coherent action – e.g. strategic planning and budgeting.
- *People and capabilities* are the talent and core competencies of the organization. This includes, for example, building a data-analytics capability by hiring data scientists, investing in analytical tools and supporting data platforms.
- *Measures and rewards* are the ways organizations measure and incentivize performance. This includes compensation and non-monetary rewards such as recognition and career advancement.
- *Culture* is the shared set of values (what we care about), beliefs (what we hold to be true) and norms of behaviour (how we do things) that shape how people behave.

Why is it helpful to think about your organization as a system? Because it allows you to diagnose and design the individual elements independently. From there, you can drive organizational change from any of the six elements. You could also develop a new strategy or restructure your organization, implement new processes (which are the foundational elements of digital transformation) or bring in people with different capabilities.

As you do this, it's essential to understand how changes in one element impact on the others and the system's overall state. Why? Because organizational systems need to have "fit" or coherence among their elements. Misalignment between elements, such as strategy and structure, can result in dysfunction and underperformance.

Suppose, for example, that a pillar of your new strategy is to make your organization more customer centric. You are unlikely to succeed if decision-making remains siloed, for example, or if the processes and data required to understand the customer aren't in place. So, while you may decide your business needs a new strategy, you must also consider what to do to transform the other elements of the organization.

Identify leverage points

Modelling business domains as systems can also help you identify potential *leverage points*. These are places in the system where modest changes create significant shifts.

Returning to the organizational system model above, you will see that culture sits in the middle, because all other elements influence it. Ways in which the different elements affect culture include:

- The purpose, vision and values of strategic direction.
- The number of layers, reporting relationships and the decision-making dimension of structure and governance.
- The ways processes and systems shape "ways of working."
- The backgrounds and skills of the most influential people.
- The incentives that result from what the organization measures and rewards.

Now, suppose you want to change the organization's culture. Understanding how these other elements impact on culture helps you identify the leverage points where you should apply effort. For example, to change behaviours, it's essential to define your goal in terms of target behaviours. Then, alter the HR systems that impact on employee behaviours – hiring, onboarding, performance management, engagement, learning and development – to reinforce them.

Focus on limiting factors

Another valuable way to leverage systems models is to use them to identify limiting factors or "binding constraints." Peter M. Senge, author of *The Fifth Discipline*, a seminal book on organizational learning, identified this "limits to growth" analysis as a classic way to apply systems analysis.[8]

The basic idea is that limits on the scarcest critical resources constrain an organization's ability to grow. This is akin to analyzing production processes to identify bottlenecks that, unless addressed, constrain output regardless of how much time and resources are devoted to other parts of the process. This is also known as the "theory of constraints," as developed by Eliyahu M. Goldratt in his book, *The Goal*.[9]

Another related idea comes from project management. Here, the speed of completing a project is constrained by the time required to complete the slowest critical task. Identifying these limiting factors, bottlenecks or critical paths in a system shows you where to focus your efforts to unlock energy, increase growth, drive productivity and reduce the time required to achieve desired results.

Recognize the impact of feedback loops

In addition to leverage points and limiting factors, it's essential to understand whether the system has feedback loops that stabilize it. Here, systems-analysis ideas about *state* and *equilibrium* are important to understand. A system's state describes the status of its most important variables at a specific time. A system is in equilibrium if its state remains stable or fluctuates within an intended set of limits. Feedback loops occur when the outputs of a system are circled back and used as inputs.

In many cases, system stability is a good thing. To return to the autonomous vehicle example, think of the subsystem that keeps a vehicle moving at a constant, desired speed. If it picks up speed too quickly (because it's going downhill), feedback triggers a reduction in engine power to reduce it. Likewise, if the vehicle slows beyond the limit that has been set (perhaps when it starts going uphill), the system produces more power. In this way, the vehicle sustains a relatively constant speed, albeit one that fluctuates between a specified range of limits.

Identifying the most important areas in which your organization needs feedback to sustain performance is essential. It's helpful, for example, to think of financial controls in organizations through the lens of feedback. If financial results start to falter, you want this to be identified early on. Once identified, attention gets focused on the issue, and corrective action can be taken. The key is to ensure the financial control system is (1) focused on measuring things that provide early warning of impending problems and (2) has feedback mechanisms that direct attention and stimulate corrective action in the right ways.

However, stability and the feedback loops that sustain it are not always good things. For example, in leading organizational transformation, efforts to drive change usually come up against forces that resist change. These "restraining forces" include rigid mindsets, fear of change, conflicting incentives and culture. Some help keep the organization stable and productive in "normal times." However, they can be severe impediments when a transformation is required to meet new challenges. Then, these forces must be overcome to move the organization to a new and better state.

Beware of non-linearities and tipping points

Finally, recognize that system dynamics usually have important non-linearities and "tipping points." When a system is linear, input changes generate proportional changes in outputs. Think of applying your foot to the accelerator of your (non-autonomous) vehicle. You apply a certain amount of pressure to the pedal, and the vehicle speed increases correspondingly. When you apply twice as much pressure, you double the speed; it's proportional. Now, imagine that your vehicle's accelerator pedal operated in a non-linear way. You push it a bit, and it speeds up by 10 per cent. Push the same amount more, and it speeds up by 100 per cent. Then by 1,000 per cent. Imagine how easy it would be to go out of control and crash.

On the other hand, sometimes the non-linearity in a system shows up as diminishing returns against the amount of energy applied to change it. To illustrate, imagine that the pressure you apply to your vehicle's brakes has a diminishing impact. You press the brake only a hair, and it slows down quite a bit, but pressing harder has less and less impact. Ultimately, you're slamming on the brakes, but the car isn't stopping. In the business world, diminishing returns may occur when you invest in improving working conditions when substandard pay levels are driving people away. Once you've provided a reasonably pleasant work environment or flexible work-from-home policies, adding a Starbucks gift card won't have much impact. So, you must stay alert to potential non-linearities in your organization's systems. Watch out for the potential for small changes beyond a certain point to generate unintended negative impacts or diminishing returns.

Tipping points, on the other hand, occur when systems that have become reasonably linear reach critical threshold states, beyond which changes develop rapidly, non-linearly and irreversibly. Climate change provides the best worst-case example of the potential dangers associated with this. Scientists are concerned that the planet's climate conditions could hit key tipping points, after which conditions on earth are projected to devolve rapidly into a much less hospitable state.

One such critical threshold involves the loss of ice at the Poles. Because ice is white, it reflects large amounts of solar radiation back out into space. As it melts, the ice is replaced by the darker soil or water beneath, which absorbs much more of the sun's heat. This process speeds further melting and accelerates the rise in global temperatures. Another critical climate threshold occurs as the Poles become warmer: scientists are concerned that large amounts of carbon dioxide and methane (an even more potent greenhouse gas), currently trapped in permafrost, will be released into the atmosphere. If this happens, it will cause global temperatures to rise even more, potentially forcing sudden, dramatic, irreversible changes in the climate system.

Thankfully, organizational changes are not nearly so complex (or potentially catastrophic). There can even be upsides to organizational tipping points. In fact, the forces resisting change from within may diminish or collapse once you achieve sufficient progress in a transformation initiative. The people who have been resisting may shift from trying (actively or passively) to block change to accepting that change will happen and deciding how to live with it, or leaving the organization.

Reflection: Does this discussion cause you to think about your organization's challenges in different, potentially valuable ways?

How do you design adaptive organizations?

In addition to modelling and making predictions, you can leverage systems analysis to design essential processes. One example is the COVID-19 vaccination effort. Billions of doses were produced and delivered across the globe at breakneck speed. One Pfizer–BioNTech COVID-19 injection contains more than 280 different ingredients. It took 25 suppliers in 19 nations to make the vaccine.[10] This was a triumph for science, drug development, and supply chain management.

Well-designed systems are *adaptive*. They recognize emerging threats (and opportunities) and adapt accordingly. Many companies underperform or fail because they've become too bureaucratic or siloed, causing delays in sensing and responding to the emergence of threats and opportunities.

To highlight how intentional systems design can help you make your organization more adaptive, consider an approach I co-developed with Amit S. Mukherjee, author of *Leading in the Digital World: How to Foster Creativity, Collaboration, and Inclusivity*. The starting point is to ask yourself some basic questions. What are the critical elements of the organizational system, and how should they connect? What are the most important feedback loops? What are the implications for the design of your organization? As Mukherjee stresses in his book, the foundation of adaptability is the capacity to *sense and respond* to changes. Not sensing changes or not doing so rapidly enough will guarantee that your organization will fail to see dangerous threats or promising opportunities, until it's too late.[11]

Detecting threats

Let's focus on how your organization senses and responds to potential threats (although similar ideas apply to identifying potential opportunities). The first thing your organization needs is a *threat-detection subsystem* that highlights changes and identifies potential danger. This subsystem must perceive important patterns and distinguish between "real" signals requiring action and background noise. Otherwise, you'll either miss essential signals and underreact, or see false signals and overreact.

This critically important subsystem consists of everything your organization does to scan the external (social, regulatory, competitive) and internal (organizational) environments, recognize potential risks and raise awareness of the need to respond. HR focuses on employee engagement and retention; government relations professionals keep on top of regulatory and legislative developments; external communications teams monitor social media; strategists focus on the actions of competitors, and so on.

Many elements of effective threat detection are likely already in place in your organization. However, you should assess whether (1) each element is as effective as it needs to be in recognizing important patterns and providing feedback as rapidly as possible; (2) these inputs are being integrated and interpreted appropriately; and (3) there are no potentially dangerous gaps in your organization's overall threat-detection coverage.

Is your organization at times surprised by threats that weren't recognized – or were, but too late? Sometimes, the threat-detection subsystem fails because the surprise is predictable but not recognized. This can happen when silos prevent information and insight from being integrated, or when incentive systems motivate people to do the wrong things. Many businesses fail because of predictable surprises rooted in organizational design weaknesses.

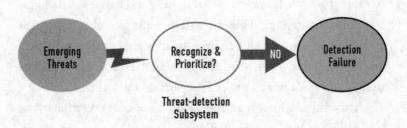

Figure 3: A threat-detection subsystem

Responding to crises

There are, of course, unpredictable surprises or "bolts from the blue" that could not have been foreseen. When sufficiently serious, they cause crises to which you and your organization must respond effectively. Crisis-management capability is, therefore, a second critical subsystem of adaptive organizations. It is the mechanism through which your organization mobilizes to act and mitigate potential damage. Often, this involves a separate set of organizational structures and processes that move the business from "normal operations" to "war-fighting" mode. This typically means implementing more centralized control to ensure rapid, coherent responses. Good crisis-management systems also have resources that are ready to go such as modular response plans that include communications protocols and scripts on the shelf ready to be used.[12] Good crisis-management systems also should be modular – for example preset scripts for communications and protocols for facility lockdowns or evacuations.

Learning from experience

After your organization has experienced a crisis, you must not simply return to business as usual; engage in a period of post-crisis learning. There should be disciplines and processes in place

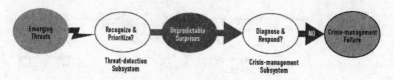

Figure 4: How a threat-detection subsystem connects
to a crisis-management subsystem

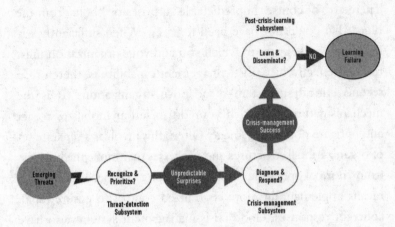

Figure 5: Incorporating a post-crisis-learning subsystem

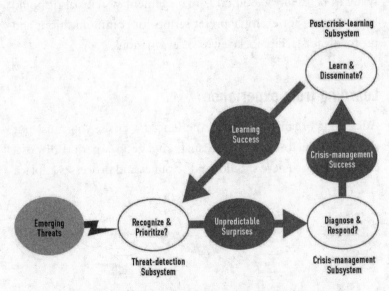

Figure 6: How learnings from a post-crisis-learning subsystem
support other subsystems within an organization

to distil and disseminate learnings to strengthen your organization's threat-detection and crisis-management subsystems for the future. This is akin to the US Army's "after-action review" process that requires commanders whose units have engaged in combat to reflect and learn. The resulting insights are gathered and collected in a repository called the "Center for Army Lessons Learned," which supports officer training.[13]

Preventing future problems

Finally, what happens when your organization's threat-detection subsystem does its job and identifies an emerging threat? To what extent is your business able not just to sense but proactively respond to avoid emerging problems and prevent crises? Your organization needs to have a problem-prevention subsystem that acts *proactively*, thereby avoiding the need to respond *reactively* (because an issue that could have been prevented wasn't and became a crisis).

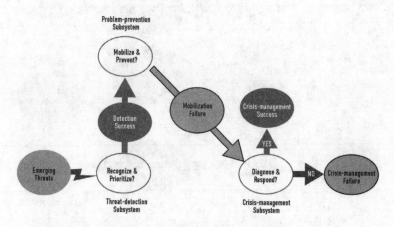

Figure 7: Incorporating a problem-prevention subsystem

In summary, to build an adaptive organization that senses and responds effectively to what is happening externally and internally, your overall system needs to have four distinct but interconnected subsystems:

- *Threat detection*: recognizing and prioritizing responses to emerging threats.
- *Crisis management*: diagnosing and responding to crisis-generating surprises.
- *Post-crisis learning*: reflecting on crises and disseminating the learnings to avoid unnecessary future problems.
- *Problem prevention*: mobilizing resources and taking action to avoid the impacts of threats that you can recognize and prioritize.

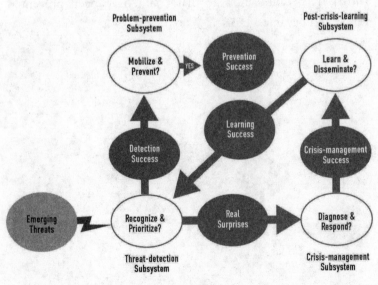

Figure 8: The four interconnected subsystems

If these subsystems are designed well and interact as intended, your organization should be positioned to thrive in our increasingly turbulent world.

While we have focused on how your organization should deal with threats, you can apply the same logic to recognizing and responding to potential opportunities. This ability to "see" emerging opportunities, and not just react to problems, is a hallmark of true strategic thinkers.

To capitalize on opportunities, you first need to be able to identify them. Then, if the opportunities you identify are promising and time-sensitive, you must pursue them quickly. Success here could make you a market leader among your competitors. If your efforts to pursue opportunities – for example, by launching a new product – fail, you want the organization to learn from those experiences. And, of course, you want your organization to pursue and capitalize on many small opportunities for improvement as part of normal operations.

Being a good strategic thinker ultimately means building up your capabilities to (1) leverage pattern recognition and systems analysis to detect challenges and opportunities; (2) deal with crises created by unpredictable surprises; (3) learn from these experiences; and (4) progressively refine your capacity to prevent problems from happening in the first place.

Reflection: What are the biggest opportunities for your organization to become more adaptive? How will you pursue them?

What are the limitations of systems analysis?

Systems models are helpful only when they capture a domain's essential features and dynamics. This is known as the *fidelity* of the model. If a model's fidelity is low, it's missing critical variables or not capturing essential dynamics. Systems models are only as good as the assumptions you make when you create them. If the model is oversimplified, it can yield dangerously wrong predictions or result in potentially severe unintended consequences.

It is therefore vital that you recognize the limits of your models. Good models are strongly correlated with the domains they represent, even if they can never represent them with 100 per cent accuracy. Your ability to make good predictions rests on having accurate and complete information and getting it in a timely matter. The human mind prefers simple, linear chains of cause and effect. However, linear models do not work well when the system's dynamics are non-linear or have tipping points. Likewise, our models can fail spectacularly when we're hit with curveballs.

Moreover, changes you don't see can cause serious problems; an out-of-date model can be worse than no model at all. In an era of rapid business change, staying alert to the need to update or discard your models is, therefore, essential. This is not simply a matter of learning new information; you must *unlearn* the obsolete models entirely. You do this by recognizing that the old model is either incomplete or ineffective. Then you find or create a fresh model that better serves your purpose. Finally, you develop new mental habits and strive to avoid the tendency to revert to the old ways of thinking.

How can you get better at systems analysis?

Like most things worth doing, getting good at systems analysis takes work. By one estimate, 95 per cent of the world's population cannot think in terms of systems because they are so used to using simple cause-and-effect chains to solve problems.[14] That so few can see the bigger picture underscores the strategic advantage that systems thinkers possess. Many will have picked up the fundamentals while in education, especially if they studied engineering or sciences. But even if you don't have that training, you're not out of luck. You likely already do some systems modelling, even if you don't describe it as such. Think back to your days in school when you learned about the water cycle: evaporation, condensation, precipitation and transpiration. In experiments, young children have developed systems-analysis abilities very quickly.[15]

Defining the boundaries of systems is the first step to modelling. Boundaries are needed to provide clarity and reduce complexity. But if they're too narrow, you might miss potential knock-on effects. Conversely, creating boundaries that are too large creates problems, too, like masking the most relevant insights in a deluge of data. There's no one-size-fits-all approach. Boundaries will be highly individualized, depending on the problem.

The next step is mapping out what happens, why it happens, and how (A causes B, C causes A, and so on). This mapping helps you understand how complex systems behave so that you might change them successfully. An excellent way to learn to think in systems terms (and thereby envision the future) is to draw *causal loop diagrams* that allow you to visualize how different elements are connected. The diagrams will deepen your understanding and allow you to better test your mental models. You can also seek input from colleagues to challenge your assumptions and make your models more rigorous.

The third step is assessing whether the system has limiting factors that could be addressed. For example, could leadership agree to a modest additional investment to build a needed capability? Next, you will need to think through different solutions and evaluate their potential effectiveness using simulations, experiments or prototypes. After an evaluation of their probable success, a decision can be made. If the solution fails, strategic thinkers will iterate this process until they achieve the desired result.

That said, making reliable predictions is incredibly difficult – if not impossible – in a world of increasing complexity. Your goal should not be to forecast your company's full range of future possibilities; instead, the ability to assess uncertainty itself is more important in today's volatile and ambiguous world. That assessment provides a vital perspective that strengthens your intuition and helps you to make better choices.

Ultimately, you will hone your ability to analyze systems through practice; business simulations are great tools. Simulations provide a manageably complex environment where you can safely experiment and gain insight into cause–effect relationships. And, unlike the real world, you can rewind things and try again if they don't work out the first time.

Summary

Systems analysis is a discipline of strategic thinking that builds on and leverages your pattern-recognition abilities. By helping you to build simplified models of the domains in which your business operates, it enables you to manage complexity better. Modelling your organization as a system allows you to think more precisely about the key elements and interactions, and better diagnose issues and design solutions. The next chapter explores a third discipline that supports modelling and helps you develop strategies: *mental agility*.

Systems Analysis Checklist

1. Are there domains in your business that are complex and challenging to understand, and if so, would it help to model them as systems?
2. Does thinking about your organization as a system help you to understand essential dynamics, diagnose problems and drive change?
3. As you think about the systems you're dealing with, what are the key leverage points, limiting factors and feedback loops?
4. Can you leverage systems analysis to make your organization more adaptive?
5. How can you enhance your ability to apply systems analysis in your organization?

To Learn More

The Fifth Discipline: The Art & Practice of The Learning Organization by Peter M. Senge

The Art of Thinking in Systems: A Crash Course in Logic, Critical Thinking and Analysis-Based Decision Making by Steven Schuster

Thinking in Systems: A Primer by Donella H. Meadows

CHAPTER 3

THE DISCIPLINE OF MENTAL AGILITY

TO BE A great strategic thinker, you must navigate the complexities of your business with agility, absorb new information, and focus on what is most relevant. Pattern recognition and systems analysis lay the foundation for developing sound strategies and adjusting them to changing circumstances. You can further amplify those abilities by mastering a third discipline: *mental agility*. It's the capacity to continually rethink the best ways to move your organization forwards amid ever-increasing complexity, uncertainty, volatility and ambiguity.

Mental agility relies on two cognitive abilities that complement and amplify one another. The first is *level-shifting*. This is the ability to explore challenging business situations using different levels of analysis – to see the forest and the trees, to foresee future developments and understand their present implications, and to move fluidly and intentionally between levels.

The second pillar of mental agility is *game-playing*. This is the ability to focus on the "games" your business needs to play, anticipate the actions of other intelligent "players," and factor them into your strategy. Every action you take prompts reactions from customers, suppliers, competitors, regulators and so on. If you're launching a new product, how will your competitors respond? What objections are regulators likely to raise if you're acquiring another business? How will your sales force react if you introduce a new incentive system?

The combination of level-shifting and game-playing allows you to recognize and respond to emerging threats and opportunities rapidly.

Learning to level-shift

Level-shifting is the ability to look at the same situation from different levels of analysis; taking the "50,000-foot view" and then "getting down to details" before shifting back up again. It's an essential element of strategic thinking. Gene Woods said:

> I tell my team that we need to be "cloud-to-ground thinkers." You can't craft a strategy without knowing what's going on in your organization and discerning whether it will enable or frustrate what you are trying to do. I often shift between the cloud and the ground several times in every strategy discussion with my team.

Likewise, level-shifting allows us to think about the now while also focusing on the future – a vital skill set. A former HR leader at a global healthcare company explains:

> When you're leading a business, there's a tendency to get pulled into the day-to-day, to get sucked into the minutiae. So, you must be able to keep a significant amount of your thinking focused on tomorrow and

doing the things that will help the business achieve the goals you've set further down the road.

Level-shifting lets you explore challenges and opportunities from multiple, complementary perspectives. It helps you to investigate every possible angle and incorporate the views of others to make better decisions. The best strategic thinkers move fluidly between levels of analysis. They can dive deeply into an issue to ensure that the people responsible for the details are doing their jobs. And they can zoom back out and think about the big picture.

Critically, they know when to move from one level to the other. As Woods says:

> You need to know when to be in the clouds and when to be on the ground. Too much time on the ground, and you get bogged down in minutiae. But if you're up in the clouds when you should be on the ground, you don't have the insight into the organization you need to inform the strategy. So, you must figure out the right altitude at which to fly.

If you cannot level-shift, you are unlikely to become a great strategic thinker. As Michael Parker, former CEO of Dow Chemical, put it:

> I have watched talented people – people with much higher IQs than mine – who have failed as leaders. They can talk brilliantly and have a great breadth of knowledge. But, while they know a lot at a high level, they don't know what's going on way down in the system.[1]

As you cultivate and leverage this skill set, take care to bring people with you on the journey. The faster your shifts between levels become, the more likely you are to leave people on your team confused. One recently appointed pharmaceutical company leader says that some of her reports were suffering from "mental whiplash" due to rapid changes in her "power of magnification." Level-shifting ability was essential to her success. She was skilled at crafting vision and strategy. But she also needed to understand the nitty-gritty details of her company's drugs, the patients that could benefit and the physicians who would prescribe them. But her staff simply couldn't follow her shifts from one level of analysis to another. "I learned," she said, "that I had to signal when I'm making a shift."

Reflection: To what extent are you good at level-shifting? Do you tend to get stuck in the clouds looking at the big picture, or caught down on the ground, mired in the details?

Playing (and winning) games

The game-playing dimension of mental agility is rooted in game theory, also known as "the science of strategy." It's about strategizing to play and win the "games" that influence the success of your business. These games involve intelligent actors, such as competitors, who make "moves" and "countermoves" as they (and you) seek to advance their agendas. Leading a business is, according to Woods, "like playing many chess games simultaneously. In the external environment of your business, the other players include politicians, regulators, competitors and customers. Some you control, some you can influence, and some are free agents. But the pieces never stand still."

The games businesses play typically involve cooperation to create value and competition to capture value. Value creation happens in games when you build alliances with other players who are pursuing complementary objectives. A classic example is an industry association whose members seek to shape regulation in ways that are good for everyone (although factions often seek somewhat different things within those associations).

Value capture, in contrast, happens whenever players compete to get the biggest shares of some fixed "pie" of economic value. One example is competitors in low-growth industries striving to maximize their returns. They usually compete on pricing and marketing. Even in highly competitive industries, however, there can still be some implicit (and legal) cooperation among firms. For example, they may resist initiating price wars that erode everyone's profitability.

Strategic thinkers must, therefore:

- Assess what types of games they are playing.
- Figure out who all the players are, and what they care about.
- Identify opportunities to create value through cooperation and to capture value through competition.
- Craft their strategies accordingly.

Applying game-theory concepts

Game theory has a mathematical foundation that has been powerfully applied, and often supported by sophisticated analytics, to business problems such as dynamic airline seat pricing. That said, many real-world business decisions cannot (yet) be modelled mathematically. Regardless, game-theory principles are indispensable arrows in the strategic thinker's quiver.

To illustrate its power, consider how you can leverage these ideas from game theory to develop your strategies. The first idea – *first-mover advantage* – comes from analysis of classic games of strategy, like chess, in which players move sequentially, and someone gets to make the first move. Does being the first mover in a game give that player an advantage? The answer in chess is *yes*. Researchers have concluded that the player who makes the first move with an equally able opponent has an inherent advantage, with an estimated win rate of between 52 and 56 per cent of all games.[2]

In business, first-mover advantage typically refers to being the first to enter a new market and, by doing so, capturing more value than competitors through higher revenues and profits over time.[3] It's a potential source of power in any game in which the order of action matters and being the first to act yields an advantage. When an industry becomes ripe for consolidation, for example, the firms that thrive often move first to make the most attractive acquisitions. The implication is this: it's essential to recognize early when you are playing a game in which it is potentially advantageous to make the first move.

This takes us back to the importance of pattern recognition. Within your organization, you can sometimes gain influence by being first to surface and frame problems. Decision-making processes in organizations are like rivers: big decisions to solve problems are powerfully shaped by earlier processes that help you find alternatives and evaluate their costs and benefits. By the time the problem and the options have been defined, the river is already flowing powerfully in its channel – and the eventual choice may be a foregone conclusion. A related microlevel example is the power that can flow from being the one who convenes and organizes a group to pursue an agenda of mutual concern.

Of course, being the first mover isn't always the best strategy. Sometimes it's better to be a "fast follower." Suppose, for example, you're leading research and development (R&D) at a pharmaceutical company, and there's a new analytical technology that could dramatically speed up the early phases of drug discovery. However, the investment required for development is substantial, and there's a significant likelihood that it won't realize its promise. You could invest in building the capability now (being a first mover) and potentially reap the competitive benefit. Or you could wait to see what happens as start-ups develop the technology and then you either acquire one of those companies or hire people to build the now-proven capability (making you a fast follower).

In many games, the players can't or don't want to communicate directly and may instead choose methods for indirect *signalling*. It's illegal in most places for competitors to collude to fix prices. However, it *is* legal for companies to decide to raise or lower prices and send signals to competitors.

To illustrate, let's start with an industry in a state of *stable equilibrium*, another important game-theory concept. Equilibrium means no players in the game have an incentive to diverge from their current strategies for creating and capturing value.[4] Let's imagine that the competitors in the industry have roughly stable market shares and profits, supported by pricing and product-development strategies that maintain the equilibrium. Let's further assume that this equilibrium is stable because divergences by any player (e.g. attempts to increase market share by reducing prices) are effectively punished.

Now, suppose that inflation suddenly flares, causing the increased prices of raw materials and labour to erode profits for all the companies in the industry. The obvious response is for everyone to raise their prices. The question is: Who will be the first? And how will competitors react? The risk, of course, is that if Company Alpha raises its prices, Company Beta may decide not to follow suit in the hope of gaining market share. So, Alpha could signal its intent by raising prices in one category of products to see if Beta follows suit. If it does, Alpha could increase prices more broadly and move the industry to a new stable equilibrium.

As mentioned previously, signalling can also be a way to deter other players from making undesirable moves. To keep with the pricing example, suppose that Company Beta decides unilaterally to cut prices on an important product category to gain market share from Company Alpha. Alpha could signal its willingness to damage overall industry profitability by making even deeper price cuts. By raising the spectre of a mutually destructive price war, Alpha could deter Beta *so long as the threat is considered credible.*

Finally, signalling is a way to make irreversible commitments and potentially prevent undesirable moves by other players. This is another form of first-mover advantage. Suppose, for example, that you lead a major manufacturer of electric vehicles. While you successfully built a solid position by being early to market, you are now facing increasing competition from both established vehicle manufacturers and private equity-funded start-ups.

Designing and producing electric vehicles requires a significant up-front investment that other players will make only if they view the risks as acceptable. So, you announce your intentions to build a large plant to manufacture batteries. Then, you back your commitment by acquiring land for the factory, seeking preliminary regulatory approvals and signing contracts with key suppliers. If you successfully convince other players that you are irreversibly committed to this course of action, you change their risk–benefit assessments in ways that may deter them from investing themselves.

Beyond deciding whether and how to make the first move (or to send signals), game theory focuses on defining the best combination of moves in the games you play – known as *sequencing*. Suppose, for example, you are leading a business unit and trying to gain support from corporate decision-makers to make a substantial acquisition. There would almost certainly be processes for assessing and vetting potential deals. But it's also essential to get political support for your agenda. So, you should think strategically about who the key decision-makers are and who else will be influential in shaping their thinking. Then, you identify a promising sequence in which to talk to stakeholders about the acquisition. In doing this, your goal is to build momentum in desired directions. Getting a key person on board may make it easier to gain support from others. As your support base broadens, the likelihood of success increases, making it easier still to recruit further supporters.

In this example, you're not playing against an adversary. In most important games, however, there are other intelligent players with whom you can cooperate to create value and compete to capture value. In such situations, you must consider how others will likely respond to your actions.

As illustrated on the next page, "game trees"[5] are valuable for clarifying your thinking about sequencing. Imagine that you're considering increasing the price of a product for which you have one major competitor, and you are the market leader.

You need to decide whether to announce a price increase. Before making this move, however, you should anticipate how your competitor could respond. For example, they could decide to leave their pricing unchanged or match your increase. You should consider how likely those actions are and what you would do in either scenario. You would try to estimate the probabilities of their actions – suppose you think there is a 50:50 chance that they will follow your lead, so the probability of each of their choices is 0.5. You would then need to assess the potential benefits of them following your lead in terms of increased profits and the potential costs of them not doing so in terms of lost market share.

This is laid out in the game tree below. As you chart the sequence of moves and countermoves, you should select the sequence that maximizes the *expected value* for your company.

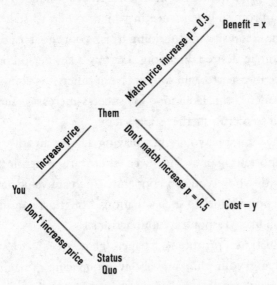

Figure 9: A game tree for clarifying thinking when considering a price increase

In this case, because you have assessed the 50:50 probabilities for your competitor's actions, the expected value of increasing your price is positive if the benefit of them also increasing their prices is greater than the cost if they don't. Expected Value = 0.5 × Benefit + 0.5 × Cost. This is > 0 if Benefit > Cost.

You can develop sequencing strategies by starting from where you are and charting a path to where you want to be, considering the potential reactions of the other players. *Backward induction*, by contrast, is about looking forwards in time to gain clarity about where you want to end up, and then reasoning backwards to the present to define your best first move. The top chess players look towards the end game, imagining how they want to be positioned and then reasoning backwards to devise the best plan for getting there.[6]

Era planning is a related discipline that draws on the logic of backward induction. The first step is to define the duration of the era: how far into the future you want to look. In these turbulent times, it's unrealistic to think you can plan with a horizon of more than two or three years. And, of course, plans may have to change drastically amidst substantial upheavals, such as a pandemic, war and severe climate events (although, as discussed in Chapter 2, it's important to foresee potential threats and develop high-level plans for dealing with them).

Once you've established the end date for era planning, the next step is to focus on two dimensions: "what will be true" and "what will be possible." To illustrate, imagine that you're planning your career development over the next three years. You have just taken a role leading sales and marketing in a mid-sized company and expect to be in this job for three years.

The "what will be true" dimension relates to what you will

have accomplished in this role at the end of the three years. To work that out, focus on what you want your legacy to be. Then apply the logic of backward induction to define what you need to do in the next six months to lay the foundation for achieving those goals.

The "what will be possible" part of era planning is about what you will do now to develop options for what you will do next. The starting point is to identify a minimum of three and a maximum of five potential futures for yourself. Try to be as clear and precise as possible about these options. Some could be natural extensions of what you're doing now – for example, becoming CEO of your current company. But it's good to develop some aspirational or "out of the box" options – for example, starting your own company. As with the "what will be true" dimension, you then apply the logic of backward induction to define how you will build bridges and create options that make these potential futures real.

You can apply this sort of backward induction/era planning logic to developing the strategy for your business. You do this by:

- Establishing your planning horizon.
- Looking ahead to "what will be true" and "what will be possible".
- Reasoning backwards to what you need to do in the shorter term to lay the foundations for achieving those goals.

This approach will also help you to develop a vision for your business, which we explore in the next chapter.

Reflection: To what extent are you good at thinking through actions and reactions in the games you and your organization need to play?

How can you develop your mental agility?

While mental agility might appear to be an innate gift, you can improve with practice. Getting better at level-shifting starts with recognizing what it is, why it's essential, and how you can improve it. Recall that we summarized strategic-thinking ability as the sum of Endowment + Experience + Exercise. Hopefully, you have or could have experiences that help you see the power of level-shifting in action, perhaps by working with established strategic thinkers. Beyond that, it's all about exercising rigorously and regularly to build a level-shifting "habit of mind." You do this by consistently looking at the situations you're dealing with from multiple points of view. Strive to combine this with work to build up your systems-analysis abilities. Any time you focus on a problem or a decision, pause and ask, "Does thinking about this in systems terms help clarify important dynamics?" If so, consciously shift between looking at the system as a whole and digging into specific elements and interconnections. As you do, watch out for tendencies to stay too high level or, conversely, to get trapped in minutiae. When this happens, intentionally try to shift yourself and others to a different level.

You can use the same basic approach to build up your ability – and your team's – to see things from current and future perspectives. It's natural to focus on the near future. So, discipline yourself to ask, "What is this situation likely to look like in a month, six months, a year?" And then, "Does looking at things from a future perspective help us think about what we need to do now?" In this way, the now vs future form of level-shifting connects to the game-playing dimension of mental agility.

Similar approaches help in developing your game-playing ability. Work on developing your ability to anticipate action and reaction. Think, if we do "A," they will likely do "B," and if we do "X," they likely will do "Y." For each chain of action and reaction, try to look a few "moves" out and then work backwards to decide on the best next steps.

Beyond exercising your mental muscles, a few other things will help develop your mental agility. Playing games like chess, even occasionally on your mobile device against virtual opponents, will help you internalize the discipline of thinking through action and reaction. Competitive card games are another opportunity to hone your ability to think through moves and countermoves. If you have the opportunity, consider playing the card game bridge online, as it will help you tune into the power of signalling. Each round of play in bridge starts with each team exchanging signals about the power of their hand and what they believe they can accomplish together through a bidding process.

When working with more complex situations or engaging in strategic thinking with teams, scenario-planning is a powerful approach for looking forwards and anticipating potential futures. The goal of scenario-planning is to broaden your scope to consider every possible scenario. This makes you more aware of your organization's threats and opportunities, so you can formulate robust strategies to cope with significant shifts in the external landscape.

If you want to build the strategic-thinking capabilities of your team, consider organizing a scenario-planning workshop. An exercise like this can promote open dialogue within your team about potential futures and their implications. Consider including people beyond your team who bring relevant expertise and viewpoints to discussions about the firm's future direction. Doing so can help catalyze creativity and innovation.

CONDUCTING A SCENARIO-PLANNING WORKSHOP

In *Scenario Thinking*, George Wright and George Cairns outline an eight-stage process for organizing a scenario workshop:[7]

1. Define the main issues about the future and set a timescale to work within to solve them. Here, it can help to interview stakeholders to understand the broader context around the issues.
2. Determine the external forces driving changes in the strategic landscape – first on an individual level to harness as many perspectives as possible, and then on a group level to clarify the key points.
3. Cluster these driving forces, which helps to make the sheer quantity of ideas easier for the human brain to digest. By uncovering the links between the forces, you can better envision how each one impacts on the outcome of the others.
4. Define two extreme but possible outcomes for each cluster of forces, then determine the relative degree of impact on the focal issue.
5. Assess the degree of uncertainty about those outcomes and test whether they are independent of one

another – and if not, combine them into one factor to broaden the range of possibilities.

6. Do a reality check of the outcomes for gaps in logic, scale and information to confirm that they still make sense.

7. Group the outcomes into best-case and worst-case scenarios, build their substance and engage in critical discussion to clarify the most plausible futures.

8. Develop these scenarios into storylines, including key events, chronological structure and the "who and why" of what happens.

The aim is to consider the external drivers of the business environment and identify threats and opportunities more clearly. From there, leaders can consider their organization's strengths and weaknesses relative to the shifting landscape.

If you decide to organize a workshop, be intentional about finding ways to deepen the dialogue. One potentially productive way is to create subgroups to debate alternatives and reach a consensus on solutions. This process is known as *dialectical inquiry*. Another approach, called *devil's advocacy*, involves having one group propose a course of action and having the other critically analyze all the elements.

Role playing is another powerful way to anticipate action and reaction through simulation of the interactions among the players in a game. Marketing expert Scott Armstrong found that role playing is most effective in making accurate predictions when the scenario is as close to the actual situation as possible. Note that it helps to role-play the interactions of the full range of stakeholders – competitors, customers, regulators and so on – as this improves predictive accuracy.

Summary

Mental agility is the ability to switch between different tasks, shift your attention and think flexibly. In strategic thinking, it's your level-shifting and game-playing capabilities. Level-shifting is the capacity to look at the same situation at different levels of analysis and to move fluidly among them. Game-playing involves learning how to assess and win the most important "games" your business needs to play with competitors. Together, they help you gain further insight and develop business strategies. The next chapter explores the fourth discipline of strategic thinking: *structured problem-solving*.

Mental agility checklist

1. When is it most important for you to look at your organization's challenges and opportunities from multiple perspectives or levels of analysis?
2. Do you know any leaders who are great at level-shifting? What can you learn from them?
3. What exercises can you do to build up your level-shifting abilities?
4. What are the most important games your organization needs to play to create value and capture value?
5. How might game theory concepts such as first-mover advantage, signalling, equilibrium, sequencing and backward induction help you to develop better strategies?

6. What is your plan for becoming better at game-playing, such as by hosting scenario-planning exercises?

To learn more

The Art of Strategy: A Game Theorist's Guide to Success in Business and Life by Avinash K. Dixit and Barry J. Nalebuff

Game Theory 101: The Complete Textbook by William Spaniel

CHAPTER 4

THE DISCIPLINE OF STRUCTURED PROBLEM-SOLVING

IN THE FIRST three chapters, we explored the three strategic-thinking disciplines that help you recognize and prioritize. Pattern recognition enables you to identify what is really important. Systems analysis helps you build simplified models of complex

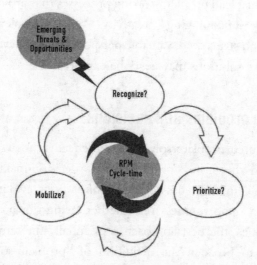

Figure 1: The recognize–prioritize–mobilize cycle

domains, amplifying your pattern-recognition abilities. Mental agility allows you to look at challenges and opportunities from different perspectives and think through actions and reactions.

The next three chapters will help you with the mobilization part of the recognize–prioritize–mobilize (RPM) cycle to deal with threats and opportunities. Structured problem-solving supports you in systematically thinking through problems and developing potential solutions. Visioning enables you to identify desirable futures and motivate your organization to realize them. Political savvy allows you to navigate internal and external politics and build alliances to implement solutions.

Let's start with structured problem-solving, a systematic approach that breaks problem-solving down into discrete steps, such as identifying key stakeholders, framing the problem, generating potential solutions, evaluating and selecting the best solution, and implementing that solution. To deal with emerging organizational challenges and opportunities, strategic thinkers must lead problem-solving processes that provide structure while encouraging creativity. When problem-solving becomes too structured, valuable perspectives may never surface and creative solutions may never be explored.

What are problems and decisions?

For structured problem-solving to be effective, it's essential to understand the terms "problem" and "decision-making." The word "problem" often has negative connotations, evoking threats rather than opportunities. Yet whether facing down threats or opportunities, the best approach is essentially the same. Hence the need to broaden the definition of "problem-solving" to encompass both the good and the bad news. "Decision-making," meanwhile, is choosing a solution to your problem from a set of mutually exclusive options by applying evaluative criteria and making trade-offs. Structured problem-solving is the process you use to develop solutions that avoid value destruction by neutralizing threats and create value by capitalizing on opportunity.

Reflection: What are the most important problems that you and your team need to solve today? What approaches do you normally take to tackle these kinds of challenges?

What's hard about "wicked big" problems?

Choosing where to go for lunch is a recurring, low-consequence problem. The high-stakes problems facing your organization, however, are another matter. These are often novel and anything but simple. This combination of novelty and complexity powerfully influences organizational problem-solving processes and how you should lead them.

By definition, you have dealt with routine problems many times in the past. Whenever routine issues arise, you grind out solutions using already-developed procedures; little judgement or creativity is required. When problems are novel, however, you cannot reach for the standard playbook. Often, it's not even clear what precisely "the problem" is. In these circumstances, defining it (also known as problem formulation, problem finding and problem framing) is an essential early phase of the process. I use the term "problem framing."

Compounding the challenge of novelty, most of the important problems your organization faces today are "wicked," which is shorthand for highly challenging, increasingly intractable problems which exhibit some combination of the CUVA factors of complexity, uncertainty, volatility and ambiguity. To recap:

- *Complexity* means your organization's problems arise in systems with many elements and interdependencies. This makes it hard to figure out cause–effect relationships, predict what will happen and identify leverage points. *To solve complex problems, you need to invest in building the best possible models of systems.*

- *Uncertainty* means you need to work with probabilities and assessments of risk when determining potential solutions and making trade-offs. This is particularly challenging when other stakeholders have different estimates of probabilities and preferences for risk. So, they may reach different conclusions about what solution is "best." *To solve problems in the face of uncertainty when multiple stakeholders are involved, it helps to establish an agreed basis for evaluating solutions and making choices in terms of probabilities and risk appetite.*

- *Volatility* means that the seriousness of an existing problem may change suddenly, becoming more or less critical. And even more important issues can arise with little warning. *When volatility is high, your organization must be able to sense changes and rapidly reassess priorities for problem-solving.*

- *Ambiguity* means there isn't a consensus among key stakeholders about what "the problem" is, or perhaps even whether there is one. It can also mean there isn't agreement on the set of potential solutions and the evaluative criteria used to assess them. *When there is ambiguity, you must negotiate among potentially competing perspectives and educate key stakeholders to gain alignment on the framing of the problem and the evaluative criteria.*

The combined impact of CUVA can make your problems seem intractable, making it essential to use a structured problem-solving process. So, focus on developing your ability to lead processes that can solve high-CUVA problems. If you can do this well, it's a competitive advantage – for you and your organization.

Reflection: Consider an important problem your organization needs to frame and solve. Which of the CUVA factors is causing the most significant challenges? What are the implications?

Leading structured problem-solving processes

Efforts to conceptualize human problem-solving go back a long way. In 1910, the American philosopher John Dewey published *How We Think*, a manual on critical thinking that laid out five phases of intellectual inquiry: recognizing a problem, defining the problem, developing a suggested solution, refining the suggestion and testing it.

This will be more complicated in an organizational context. The process, therefore, tends to be a collective effort. In addition, the implementation of "solutions" usually involves substantial commitment of resources. Organizational problem-solving thus diverges from Dewey's straightforward process of intellectual inquiry in some fundamental ways.

Let's assume that you have recognized a significant emerging problem, prioritized it, and now want to mobilize resources to frame and solve it. How should you approach doing that? Conceptualize organizational problem-solving in terms of the five phases shown below. For each phase, there are some questions to help guide you on what to do:

Phase 1: Define roles and communicate the process

- Who must be involved in the problem-solving process, and in what roles?
- How should you communicate the process, and what are the implications?

Phase 2: Frame the problem

- How can you define the problem as a specific question to be investigated?
- What criteria will be used to evaluate the fitness of potential solutions?
- What are the biggest obstacles you anticipate needing to overcome?

Phase 3: Explore potential solutions

- What is a complete set of promising potential solutions?
- What approach will you use to identify or develop the different options?

Phase 4: Decide on the best option

- Given your evaluative criteria, what is the best option to solve the problem?
- How will you deal with any significant uncertainties?

Phase 5: Commit to a course of action

- What resources need to be allocated to implement the solution?
- What needs to be done, and by whom?

Once you have "solved" a significant problem and committed to a path forward, you will likely need to frame and solve additional problems. That is why our five-phase process is shown as a cycle in Figure 10, below. Success in completing one cycle often generates more problems to solve.

In the middle of the figure is a reminder that you should strive to balance the two halves of the brain: the left-brain dimension is more structured, while the right brain is more creative. Creativity can play a role in all five phases of the process but being structured is essential throughout.

Reflection: How do you engage in structured problem-solving today? What are the strengths and weaknesses of your current approach?

To illustrate structured problem-solving in action, consider the strategy-development work Gene Woods undertook soon after he became CEO at CHS. Recall that Woods inherited a successful,

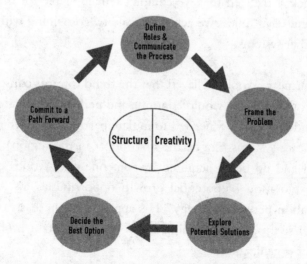

Figure 10: The five-phase cycle of organizational problem-solving

modest-sized healthcare system. In part, CHS had built its success by contracting with nearby healthcare systems to provide management services, such as back-office payment processing. In 2016, these relationships generated about $3 billion in annual revenue in addition to the $5 billion CHS generated internally. The organization gained a scale and breadth of geographic scope that increased its power in negotiating with suppliers and insurers.

Woods believed, however, that CHS's management services business model was under threat:

> What I realized is that none of these relationships had a pathway towards true integration. So, we were leaving a lot of value on the table. We were also propping up some weaker systems. Paradoxically, this allowed them to negotiate harder with us when the management services contracts came up for renewal, as many of them did soon after I became CEO . . . When I took a step back, I realized that we couldn't remain viable for the long-term unless we achieved scale by combining with other systems.

Furthermore, Woods believed that the trend towards consolidation in the industry would continue and perhaps accelerate. He concluded that CHS needed to initiate partnerships with other healthcare systems (i.e. be the first mover in the region), or it would end up being acquired by someone else. Woods called this exploration of potential growth opportunities his "next-generation network strategy." His approach is the basis of the five-phase process for framing and solving important problems in your organization.

Phase 1: Define roles and communicate the process

Most executives will need to involve their leadership team and others in the process. That adds complexity, given they are usually people, groups or organizations who (1) have a stake in the problem you're grappling with and (2) influence your ability to frame and solve it. As Woods developed his next-generation network strategy for Atrium Health, for example, he needed to regularly engage with his board of directors. To engage most effectively with stakeholders, you first need to identify them. Then, you should decide how to involve them by applying a simple framework of Approve, Support, Consult and Inform – or ASCI for short.[1]

- *Approve*: You need their formal approval to make key decisions or commitments. Woods knew, for example, that any significant deal to combine with another healthcare system would require approvals from the state and federal government agencies overseeing antitrust regulation.
- *Support*: They control resources – people, funding, information, relationships – that you need. In addition to needing his board's approval for any potential deal, Woods also needed their support to fund key activities.
- *Consult*: It's valuable to have them on board, or you want to get their input on critical issues, or both. They may also be stakeholders whom you anticipate will be in the "Approve" or "Support" columns for later phases of the process, so you want to engage them early on.
- *Inform*: You need to keep them up to date on progress using only one-way communication. Often, this is because they will play more active roles in subsequent phases of the process.

Before embarking on your problem-solving process, complete an ASCI matrix. Identify the key stakeholders and the roles you anticipate they will play in each stage of the journey. Plan to update the matrix as the process unfolds; your understanding of stakeholders and their roles will undoubtedly evolve as you learn more. To get you started, the matrix below summarizes the stakeholders that Woods needed to engage.

ASCI matrix for Atrium Health's Next-Generation Network Strategy

The next step is to communicate the problem you are trying to solve to your stakeholders. Informing them about your goals

	Approve	Support	Consult	Inform
Phase 1. Define roles and design the process	• Board of directors	• Board of directors • Chief of staff • CFO • General counsel	• Government relations staff	• Leaders responsible for existing relationships with other systems
Phase 2. Frame the problem		• Executive team		
Phase 3. Explore potential solutions		• Extended leadership team	• Key organizational thought leaders • External consultants	
Phase 4. Decide on the best option	• Board of directors	• Extended leadership team	• Key organizational thought leaders • External consultants	• Organizational leaders engaged in strategy execution
Phase 5. Commit to a course of action	• Board of directors • State and federal government regulators	• External legal and regulatory advisors	• Organizational leaders engaged in strategy execution	

helps them make sense of what's happening. Additionally, the "power of fair process" can help you to gain buy-in as you progress from phase to phase. Research has shown that people are more likely to accept outcomes that are not wholly favourable to them if they perceive the decision-making process to be fair.[2] In the context of structured problem-solving, this means being transparent about the process.

Reflection: Have there been situations in the past when you've struggled to solve problems because you didn't engage with stakeholders early enough?

Phase 2: Frame the problem

When problems are novel, and especially when they are wicked, it's essential to be rigorous in framing them. In fact, this may be the most important phase of the entire process. As Albert Einstein and Leopold Infeld put it in *The Evolution of Physics*:

> The formulation of a problem is often more essential than its solution, which may be merely a matter of mathematical or experimental skill. To raise new questions, new possibilities, to regard old problems from a new angle requires creative imagination and marks real advance in science.[3]

Framing a problem means:

1. Defining the problem in the form of a question that needs to be answered.
2. Clarifying the criteria that will be used to evaluate the fitness of potential solutions.

3. Identifying the most significant potential barriers that must be overcome to succeed.

That may seem like a lot to do up front, but it will save time when you come to solving the problem. In their excellent book *Solvable*, Arnaud Chevallier and Albrecht Enders introduce a powerful approach to framing problems that leverages the storytelling construct of the "Hero's Journey" (think Luke Skywalker in *Star Wars*).[4] They encourage leaders to frame problems in terms of a *hero* who embarks on a *quest* seeking a *treasure* during which they must defeat one or more *dragons*.

Who or what are the hero, the quest, the treasure and the dragons?

- The *hero*, of course, is you, the leader, framing and solving a significant organizational problem.
- The *quest* is the reason you need to go on the journey, *in the form of a question that clearly defines the problem*.
- The *treasure* is the best possible solution, and the benefits of realizing it.
- The *dragons* are the potential barriers you must confront and surmount along the road.

Enders and Chevallier's framework is helpful because it memorably distils your thinking. *It's especially valuable when problem-solving involves multiple stakeholders*. Why? Because the framework is a "shared language" that helps you to align stakeholders with divergent views of the problem, the potential solutions and the criteria for evaluating them. Striking agreements on the definitions of the quest, the treasure and dragons can help you manage your stakeholders more effectively.

The first step in framing is to *precisely define the quest in the form of a question that crystallizes the problem*. In doing so, it's essential to "size" the problem, which means striking a balance between being overly ambitious and not ambitious enough. If you try to "boil the ocean," or make the project unnecessarily difficult, you set yourself up for failure. Likewise, you're destined for disappointment if you focus on figuring out "how many angels can dance on the head of a pin." The right level of ambition lies somewhere between the ocean and the angels.

As you define the problem, be both strategic and creative. Being strategic means understanding the full set of stakeholder interests and defining the problem in ways that consider them. Being creative means understanding and leveraging biases in how people think to move things forward.

Enders and Chevallier give a witty example of creativity in problem-framing:

> Two monks living in an abbey want to be able to smoke tobacco while they pray. The impact likely will be more praying but less concentration when doing so, so it's hard to evaluate whether there is a net benefit. The first goes to the abbot and asks, "Is it OK if I smoke while I pray?" and gets rebuffed. The second monk does the same but asks the abbot, "Is it OK if I pray while I smoke?" and gets permission.[5]

This underscores how people think about gains and losses, specifically the well-established decision-making bias known as *loss aversion*. Research in cognitive psychology has shown that people care more deeply about avoiding losses than achieving equivalent gains.[6] The first monk framed his request in a way that highlighted potential losses for the abbot – smoking while praying could impair average prayer quality. The second monk emphasized the potential gains for the abbot – being allowed to smoke while praying could result in more praying.

This takes us to the second step you'll use in framing: *specifying the criteria used to evaluate potential solutions*. Evaluative criteria help you answer the questions:

- What must be true about an acceptable solution to the problem (i.e. the treasure)?
- How will potential solutions be assessed in terms of their relative attractiveness?

You should identify a set of criteria that are distinct, compact and reasonably comprehensive. If you're deciding which restaurant to go to, for example, "tastes good," "is satisfying" and

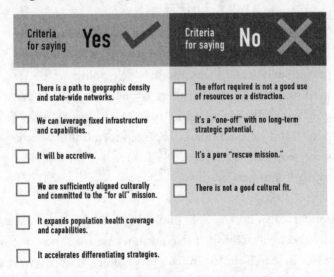

Figure 11: Woods's evaluative criteria

"leaves me feeling good" are too generic and vague to be used as evaluative criteria. Strive also to identify the most important yardsticks. Too many evaluative criteria bring diminishing returns. With the support of his leadership team, Woods defined the criteria in Figure 11, below, to evaluate potential deals with other healthcare systems.

The third step and final element of good problem-framing is to *identify the barriers that are likely to stand in your way as you pursue the treasure*. It helps to anticipate obstacles before you move on to exploring solutions, evaluating options and making decisions. Woods saw his three dragons as the following:

1. Helping the people on his team get comfortable with ambiguity and give up on needing a defined strategy up front.
2. Convincing his board and other key stakeholders that Atrium Health "needed to grow differently despite the success of the old model."
3. Restructuring his leadership team and adding the talent needed to drive the new approach.

Reflection: Think of a significant organizational problem you need to solve. Is the problem framed adequately? Would it help to use Enders and Chevallier's framework to align stakeholders?

Phase 3: Explore potential solutions

It's wise to separate the exploration of potential solutions from the evaluation of those solutions. Why? Because finding solutions to wicked problems often requires creativity, ingenuity and vision, while selecting among them is about hard-headed analysis. Premature critical evaluation tends to squash creativity. As

Michael A. Roberto puts it in *Unlocking Creativity*, "Unfortunately, the failure to manage dissent and contrarian perspectives constructively causes many good ideas to wither on the vine."[7]

Start by identifying the type of exploration in which you need to engage. The most straightforward situations arise when the possible solutions are fixed and obvious. Returning to our hypothetical case of deciding where to go for a quick lunch, we know the neighbourhood, how much time we have, and hence what options are immediately available. So, there's no need for exploration at all! When the set of potential solutions is obvious, you can skip directly to evaluation. Unless existing restaurants close or new ones open, your options are fixed, and you can focus on planning.

When solutions are not obvious but are likely to exist, then your exploration is about *efficient search*. You devote resources to looking for potential solutions. You continue until you have discovered all possible options. However, when searching is costly or time-consuming, you define a *stopping rule*. This means you search until you've identified a set of plausible options and then shift to a more rigorous evaluation. (Note that stopping after finding just one potential solution violates the rule of separating exploration and evaluation but is sometimes justified when you're under time pressure.)

If you cannot find any good solutions, you need to break down the problem. That involves applying analytical tools such as systems modelling (discussed in Chapter 2) and root-cause analysis to explore the underlying drivers and identify the easy fixes and most challenging subproblems. You can then build up potential solutions creatively. Root-cause analysis involves breaking the problem into more detailed pieces. Its power is illustrated in Figure 12, which charts how to diagnose the causes of shipping delays at a manufacturing facility.

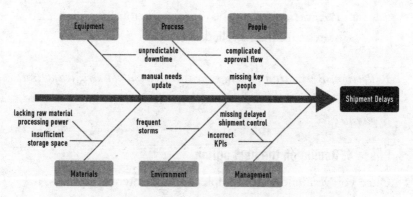

Figure 12: Root-cause analysis to diagnose the
causes of shipping delays

The diagram categorizes the potential causes of the problem into logical categories such as equipment, materials and processes. That can help you to find quick fixes and develop new approaches to solving a problem (or subproblems like reducing equipment downtime). To do that, you need to find creative talent and motivate them. For example, don't impose too much structure or overly constrain the process. Beyond that, provide the space and time for creative thought to unfold. In his book *The Art of Thought*, Graham Wallas highlights the importance of time in his five-stage model for unleashing creativity:[8]

1. *Preparation*: When the creative individual's mind is on the problem and explores its dimensions.
2. *Incubation*: When the problem is internalized in the unconscious mind.
3. *Intimation*: When the creative person gets a "feeling" that a solution is on its way.
4. *Illumination*: When the creative idea bursts forth from preconscious processing into conscious awareness.

5. *Verification*: When the idea is consciously verified, elaborated and then applied.

Reflection: Returning to a significant problem you are grappling with, what approaches to exploring potential solutions do you need to pursue?

Phase 4: Decide on the best option

Once you've identified a complete set of potential options, the next step is to evaluate them rigorously and pick the best one. When the criteria are equally important, your evaluation of them is a simple "Yes" or "No." Often, however, evaluation is about *making trade-offs*. Returning to the decision about where to go for lunch, imagine that you use just two evaluative criteria – taste and time – to choose a restaurant. Suppose you love the taste of Italian food much more than Mexican food. However, going to the Italian restaurant will take substantially more time. To what extent are you willing to take more time to gain more enjoyment from the meal? You're probably willing to devote five more minutes. But would you wait an extra hour? Probably not. Twenty minutes? Maybe. Welcome to the world of trade-offs.

When your criteria are measurable and can be converted to a common currency – for example, time or money – it's relatively easy to make trade-offs. It's far more challenging when assessments are qualitative. When this is the case, consider developing a *scoring system*. As discussed in "Scoring a Deal," a Columbia Business School case study about complex negotiations,[9] you can do this by:

- Defining the dimensions on which you will assess the options (already done as part of framing the problem).

- For each dimension, ranking your options from worst to best.
- For each dimension, creating a scale from 0 to 100 (100 being the most effective), then placing your options on the scale.
- Assigning "weights" to the dimensions in terms of their relative importance to your strategy – the weights should total one (if you have four dimensions, for example, you could assign weights of 0.3, 0.2, 0.4 and 0.1).
- Calculating the total value for each option by multiplying its score on each dimension by the weight given to the dimension, and then adding up the result.

To continue with our restaurant example, let's assume you developed the scoring summary below. Your evaluative criteria are taste, cost, total time required and nutritional value. The local Thai, Mexican and Italian restaurants are your options.

Scoring system for choosing a restaurant

Before looking at the total score, consider the weights assigned to the four dimensions of taste, cost, time and nutritional value, and recall that they must add up to one. Here, you have given quite a bit of weight to time, some to taste and cost, and a little to nutritional value. (Clearly, your health isn't a big concern right now.)

Now, look at the scores assigned to each restaurant on the dimensions of cost and taste. Recall that the scale for each dimension is 0 to 100. On the cost dimension, you've assessed the Mexican restaurant as the least expensive (score = 100), although the Thai place is a close second (score = 90), while the Italian is substantially more costly (score = 70). However, on the

	Taste	Cost	Time	Nutritional Value	Total Score
Weights (totaling 1)	0.3	0.2	0.4	0.1	
Thai	90	90	85	90	88
Mexican	70	100	100	50	86
Italian	100	70	40	100	78

taste dimension, Italian food is your favourite (score = 100), followed closely by Thai (score = 90), with Mexican food being substantially less satisfying (score = 70).

Finally, note the total scores for each option. Although you haven't ranked the Thai restaurant as your most preferred on any of the dimensions, it comes out on top in this analysis. Why? Because it's good on several important dimensions. This underscores how rigorous assessment of trade-offs can yield an unexpected "best" outcome.

Before you start applying this sort of scoring analysis to your decision-making, you must understand its limitations. First, this approach assumes you can have an array of options on linear 0 to 100 evaluation scales such as taste and time. In reality, there may be important non-linearities. Suppose, for example, you had only 30 minutes to have lunch before an important client meeting. How would that change your assessment if it takes 40 minutes to go to the Thai restaurant?

Another limitation is that the comparison of alternatives is *additive*. In other words, it assumes that you can calculate the total value of options by adding up the weighted scores. This works when there aren't important interactions among scores on two or more dimensions, which often is not the case.

This is not to say that the scoring system isn't helpful. Using this approach *can* help inform your thinking, but it must be treated as advisory and not determinative. Look at the results and ask, *Does this feel right? Did we assign the correct weights to the dimensions and scores to the options? Are there non-linearities or interactions among dimensions we must consider?*

It's also possible to create more sophisticated scores by incorporating uncertainty and assigning probabilities to outcomes associated with different choices. For example, suppose you can count on the Mexican restaurant serving you in 10 minutes, but the Thai place varies from 5 to 25 minutes. If you can assign probabilities to different wait times, you can evaluate options on an *expected-value basis*, providing a more rigorous assessment.

Finally, it's best to create a scoring system while framing the problem and not when you are evaluating your options. Doing so will help you be more objective because you won't be defining weights and assigning scores when you already know the options and may already have made informal assessments of them.

Reflection: How do you approach evaluating potential solutions to important problems today? Are you and your organization sufficiently rigorous?

Phase 5: Commit to a course of action

Finally, your solutions to organizational problems are not "answers" per se; they are *paths forward* that you commit your organization to. Robust solutions, therefore, consist of goals, strategies, plans and resource commitments. When you converge on a solution to a significant problem, you must often make substantial, irreversible resource commitments to implement it. Beyond the direct costs of pursuing a particular course of action, there may be opportunity costs of the roads not taken.

If you're disappointed with the food at the Thai restaurant,

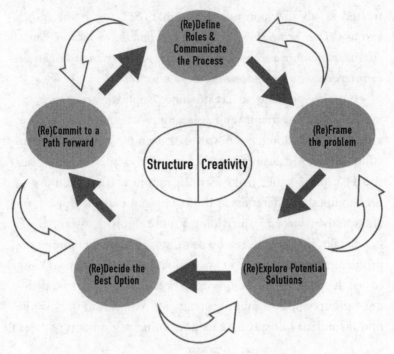

Figure 13: Moving in both directions through the five-phase
cycle of organizational problem-solving

you might experience a fleeting "I knew I should have gone for Italian," quickly assuaged with, "Oh well, I'll go there tomorrow." The consequences of failing to solve major organizational problems are, of course, far greater. The good news is that paths can often be adjusted to some extent as the situation evolves and more is learned. That process can also reveal unexpected problems that become focal points for additional problem-solving, continuing the cycle. You may need to move backwards and forwards as you progress through the process, as illustrated in Figure 13.

Reflection: How successful has your organization been in implementing solutions to complex problems?

Developing your structured problem-solving abilities

To get better at structured problem-solving, start by learning the basic principles, such as the steps in the problem-solving process, the tools and techniques used in each step, and the common pitfalls and challenges. Structured problem-solving improves with experience. The more you practise, the better you will become at it. This can involve working on a variety of problems and seeking feedback and guidance from others. Look too for opportunities to get involved in structured problem-solving processes being run by people with more experience.

Summary

Structured problem-solving is the strategic-thinking discipline that guides you in how to solve your organization's most important challenges. The process consists of discrete steps: identifying key stakeholders, framing the problem, generating potential solutions, evaluating and selecting the best solution, and implementing that solution. Part of the power of structured problem-solving lies in how it helps you to align stakeholders in pursuing your quest. The next chapter focuses on *visioning*, a discipline that helps you envision and realize attractive potential futures.

Structured Problem-Solving Checklist

1. How effective is your organization at defining and solving its most significant problems today? What are its strengths and weaknesses?

2. How should you approach engaging with key stake-holders early in the process? Would it help to do an Approve-Support-Consult-Inform (ASCI) assessment?
3. What can you do to improve your effectiveness in framing problems, including defining and communicating the quest, the treasure and the dragons to your team?
4. Do you balance analysis and creativity effectively in generating options?
5. Are you being sufficiently rigorous and making the right trade-offs in your evaluation?

To Learn More

Solvable: A Simple Solution to Complex Problems by Arnaud Chevallier and Albrecht Enders

The Art of Critical Decision Making by Michael A. Roberto

Leading in the Digital World: How to Foster Creativity, Collaboration, and Inclusivity by Amit S. Mukherjee

CHAPTER 5

THE DISCIPLINE OF VISIONING

VISIONING IS THE ability to imagine potential futures that are ambitious and achievable and then mobilize your organization to realize them. The discipline of visioning is about building bridges between potential futures and current realities. It's not enough to envision a desirable future; you must communicate and energize people around the vision. That's where what we call "powerful simplification" connects with visioning – you must articulate your vision (and the strategies that will achieve it) clearly and compellingly.

What is vision?

For business leaders, vision is a compelling mental picture of how the organization will look and feel when the strategy is fully realized. A good vision defines a future that is meaningful and attractive. A vision should answer the question: Given what this organization has to do (the mission), given its priorities (the core objectives) and given how it expects to move forwards (the strategy), what will it look like and how will people act when its vision is fulfilled?

In one leader's words, a vision is a "picture of the future distilled down to its crystalline, simplest form." Another pointed out that a vision must be descriptive and specific, explaining: "A vision describes the way the organization is going to work in a reasonable time frame in the future but [which] stretches the organization, because if they're not stretching, it's not a vision."

It's important to distinguish vision from related concepts such as mission, core objectives and strategy. To do so requires understanding of what a vision is *not*:

- A vision is not a mission, which is what the organization's leaders want the organization to do and be known for doing.
- A vision is not a set of core objectives, which are the priorities that define the targets for the mission.
- A vision is not a strategy, which lays out a general path by which the mission and core objectives will be realized.

Of course, your organization's vision must be consistent with its mission, core objectives and strategy. Something that causes substantial and positive change rarely happens without a strong meaning, purpose and vision being connective and cohesive. One of the leaders I interviewed put it this way, "People must be able to say, 'Oh, I see how all this [mission, objectives, strategy] fits together. I see where we're going.'"

It's particularly important to distinguish vision from purpose, another important element of alignment in organizations. As Peter M. Senge puts it, "Vision is different from purpose. Purpose is a general heading. Vision is a specific destination, a picture of a desired future. Purpose is 'advancing man's capability to explore the heavens.' Vision is 'a man on the moon by the end of the 1960s.'"[1]

Purpose and vision go together. A powerful purpose without a vision will leave your organization without a clear destination, ill-equipped to chart a path through the choppy waters of the CUVA world. Even if passionate individuals work tirelessly towards an aim, often what they achieve won't last, doesn't go far enough or falls short of its potential. But instilling a shared vision throughout your organization can align behaviour, pull employees towards a desirable future and temper anxiety about the uncertain world.

Why is visioning important?

Empty statements of corporate intent risk reducing vision to cliché. "Mendacity and misrepresentation" were two conclusions drawn by Chris Bart, a former professor at McMaster University's DeGroote School of Business, in a 1997 paper entitled "Sex, Lies, and Mission Statements." Bart concluded, "the vast majority [of mission statements] are not worth the paper they are written on."[2] The former West German chancellor Helmut Schmidt went further. When asked about his big vision, he said, "Anyone who has visions should go to the doctor."[3]

But visioning is an essential discipline of strategic thinking. As former Johnson & Johnson executive Troy Taylor notes, "Visioning is helping the organization understand where you want to go, what you have to do to get there, and what life is going to be like when you arrive." A compelling vision generates directed passion. You might develop the best strategy in the world, but if your people don't understand *why* action is necessary, *where* you will go, *what* needs to be accomplished and *how* it will be achieved, your strategy is useless. Visioning provides a clear picture of the "why" and the "where" through communication that distils, informs and inspires.

Done well, a vision organizes and motivates your people to pursue a common goal. Visionary leaders provide inspiring aims that help organizations overcome self-interest and factionalism. History provides ample examples. Nelson Mandela was an extraordinary political leader who overcame conflict and galvanized people to a common cause with his vision to unite South Africa across racial and political divides.

In business, visionary leaders energize their organizations. A compelling vision helps employees understand how their work contributes to the enterprise's success and furthers its mission and purpose. This can yield enormous benefits. It's even better when the vision aligns with employees' personal values. Research shows that employees are willing to sacrifice future earnings for work they feel is meaningful. In addition, employees who find their work meaningful are also 69 per cent less likely to quit, potentially saving organizations vast sums in turnover costs.[4] A related study of more than 50,000 employees shows that staff who see their company's vision as meaningful have engagement levels 18 percentage points above average.[5]

Moreover, visioning supports the essential work you must do to build alliances, which we discuss in the next chapter. Visioning enables leaders to form personal relationships and build the networks that lay the foundations for individual, team and organizational success. This is especially helpful for newly appointed CEOs, who will be looking to win over stakeholders, create excitement around their strategy and build crucial early momentum. Effective visioning, therefore, can reduce the risks of leadership transitions, especially for companies that appoint CEOs from outside the organization. Those outsider bosses tend to underperform if stakeholders are unimpressed, sceptical or disgruntled early on.

Reflection: What is the best example of effective visioning you've experienced? Have you seen cases where efforts to create a shared vision have failed? If so, why did that happen?

How do you develop a vision?

One type of visioning involves looking forwards then reasoning backwards. The logic is similar to backward induction in game theory, as discussed in Chapter 3; you look forwards in time, visualize a desirable future state, then work backwards to define what it will take to get there. Alternatively, you can take stock and imagine the possibilities. You do this by taking an inventory of your available resources and envisioning what you can achieve with them – a process termed "effectuation" in research about entrepreneurship.[6] What have we got today, and what do we already do well that we can build upon?

Regardless of whether you work backwards or forwards, the goal is to imagine potential futures that are ambitious but also achievable. Ambition is essential because realizing the vision needs to be a stretch for your team and organization. In *Built to Last*, Jim Collins and Jerry I. Porras coined the term "BHAG" – for Big, Hairy, Audacious Goal – to capture the need for vision and ambition to go together.[7]

But your vision can't be seen as "pie in the sky" or very unlikely to be realized. President John F. Kennedy's challenge to Americans in his 1961 inaugural address – to put a man on the moon before the end of the decade[8] – met both criteria, but only just (the first landing happened in July 1969[9]). Kennedy's example underscores the importance of building flexibility into a vision to create options should you hit insurmountable obstacles. Think about what happens when you frustrate the GPS in your car. If you miss a turn, the system will suggest you make a 180-degree turn and get back on track. But if you ignore its suggestions, the system comes up with a new route to the same destination. This mirrors the visioning discipline of strategic thinking in action.

From personal vision to shared vision

To create a shared vision, you should first develop a personal vision. Can you imagine a clear, desirable future state that you want to lead your business to? In addition to being an achievable goal, it must be consistent with your leadership style and situational context. Often, it's valuable to test your personal vision with people you trust.

It can help to link your vision to your core objectives. This makes it more action-orientated and tangible than if it's based solely on the firm's core values. Those core values, such as loyalty, commitment, dignity and integrity, give your vision its meaning and sense of purpose and can help to deepen the impact of your vision.

It also helps to base your vision on some well-recognized motivators. According to the late American psychologist David McClelland, people are driven by the needs for achievement (the desire to compete, perform better or win), affiliation (to identify with a social group or be part of a team) and power (the search for status or control).[10] A vision can articulate how a strategy will meet some of these needs, motivating your team more effectively. Additional examples of motivational drivers that can be evoked by well-crafted visions are shown in Figure 14, below.

Once you have a rough draft, test and refine your ideas by discussing them with a broad range of stakeholders who can subject your vision to scrutiny, searching for gaps or flaws. As the vision goes through stages of clarification, testing and refinement, it will eventually evolve into a shared narrative for success.

In some cases, it makes sense to involve others – such as your leadership team or the broader organization – in co-creating the vision. As Paul Culleton, the former head of talent management at Johnson & Johnson, says, "Creating a simple yet compelling vision is vital. If you can couple a visionary exercise together with gaining knowledge of how the people are with one another . . . that's a good place to start."

You do it when it makes sense, and sometimes it doesn't. Specifically, you should only do so when you can develop a vision that truly inspires your organization. This may not be the case if your business is making redundancies. Also important is whether people's involvement in creating the vision will increase

Motivational drivers that can be used to construct a compelling vision:

{
1. Feeling committed to something
2. Making a contribution
3. Embodying trust and integrity
4. Achieving great results
5. Being part of a team
6. Having control of our destiny
}

Figure 14: Motivational drivers

their commitment to achieving it. If so, the benefits may out-weigh the potential costs of compromising on elements of your personal vision.

If you decide to take the co-creation route, be careful not to let the audacity inherent in a great vision get watered down. It's important to be clear on the core elements of your vision that are non-negotiable. But beyond these inviolate elements, be flexible in incorporating the ideas of others so they share owner-ship. Gene Woods exemplifies the power of this "co-creation" approach. Instead of a top-down approach, he started with an intensive bottom-up listening exercise. Woods explains, "I spent a lot of time walking the halls, asking people what we do well, what should our aspirations be and what gets in the way. I also spoke with key community leaders about their perceptions of our strengths and opportunities."

As Woods went through this process, specific themes began to emerge. One was how thirsty individuals were to connect their roles to the organization's broader purpose. "Teammates wanted to keep people healthy, not just treat them when they're sick," he says. "[They] wanted to tell stories about how we pro-vide hope in people's darkest moments. [They] wanted to be national leaders [and] advance healing."

He synthesized the feedback and communicated it to key stakeholders authentically and organically. The result was a new mission statement: *To improve health, elevate hope and advance healing – for all.* The "for all" part was critical because it affirmed the company's commitment both to privileged patients (those with a choice of healthcare) and to society's most vulnerable.

Woods used a similar process to create Atrium Health's vision statement: *To be the first and best choice for care.* "This struck a chord in the organization and became a rallying cry," said Woods. "The mission reflected our heart, vision, intellect and spirit. The vision signalled a more intentional orientation towards growth and change. [It] defined how we would know we were being successful."

As Woods's experience illustrates, a good vision is clear and specific, provides meaning and passion, and relates to other key tools for establishing direction, such as the mission statement. It paints a vivid picture of the desired future: one that's consistent with the mission, core objectives and strategy of the company it depicts. Critically, it aligns the aspirations of the employees and the wider organization.

As Brad Neilley, former vice president of human resources at Johnson & Johnson, put it, "To be visionary is to have a picture of where you want the organization to go down the road. It means showing people a clear picture of what that looks like, so they understand where we're going as an organization."

Reflection: As you think about your past efforts to create a shared vision, what worked well and what didn't?

The importance of powerful simplification

To galvanize people behind the vision, you must seek to achieve *powerful simplification* by communicating your organization's future direction in straightforward, evocative terms.[11] The need to get people on board with your vision may seem self-evident, but knowing it and doing it are different things. Many leaders struggle with visioning as they move to more senior roles. Peter Tattle, former commercial head of Johnson & Johnson's pharmaceutical business, noted, "Leading an entire business may be the first time you're challenged with having such a broad perspective.

Your job is to be able to describe it in straightforward terms, in an engaging fashion, and get people to rally behind your vision of what that can become."

It often helps to create stories and develop metaphors to support your vision. Stories and metaphors are potent ways to communicate the threats and opportunities on the horizon and the strategies you will use to manage them. As the American psychologist Howard Gardner states in *Leading Minds*, "Leaders achieve their effectiveness chiefly through the stories they relate . . . In addition to communicating stories, leaders embody those stories . . . [and] convey their stories by the kinds of lives they, themselves, lead."[12] Consider this vision statement for an eyecare business: *Vision for life*. It evokes how eyesight develops and changes over a lifetime and helps connect the organization more closely to the experience of its patients.

Telling stories is one important way that leaders influence and inspire. Stories help create a sense of connection and build familiarity and trust in ways that data points cannot. Stories also stick in our minds. We can recall information in stories more accurately and for far longer than information gleaned from facts and figures. As Kendall Haven, author of *Story Proof* and *Story Smart*, notes, "Your goal in every communication is to influence your target audience (change their current attitudes, beliefs, knowledge, and behaviour). Information alone rarely changes any of these. Research confirms well-designed stories are the most effective vehicle for influencing."[13]

The best stories distil core lessons – mistakes make for good narrative fodder – and provide models for the kind of behaviour you want to encourage. Vision stories should also resonate with the older mythology of the company, drawing on the best elements of what was and combining them with what the organization might become. This process is beneficïal not just for communicating the vision but for framing strategy and other essential elements that establish the overall direction of the business.

Leaders can deliver key insights using five classic story archetypes. These are *love* (say the company has fallen in love with its product or service and wants to share its passion), *redemption* (say the business has fallen on hard times and seeks to recover), *rags to riches* (the company is an underdog looking to overcome adversity), *stranger in a strange land* (you could be launching a new product or service) and *the holy grail* (you have ambitious goals to discover deep fulfilment).[14]

Take, for example, CHS's vision to *improve health, elevate hope and advance healing – for all*. In this case, the company conforms to the love story archetype since it wants to serve customers at the highest level. By emphasizing this, the organization can harness the power of audience-centred speaking.

Repetition can also make for persuasive communication, based on findings from social psychology that show how repeated exposure to a stimulus enhances positive feelings towards it. This is known as the *exposure effect*.[15] Research also shows that it can help to express your vision in different modalities – in a speech, a letter or video – to help the message sink in. According to the American educator Edgar Dale's Cone of Experience model, we tend to remember just 10 per cent of what we read, 20 per cent of what we hear and 30 per cent of what we see. Knowledge retention rises to 50 per cent of what we hear and see simultaneously (e.g. through a video) and 70 per cent of what we say and write, such as if we're participating in a discussion and taking notes. The retention rises to 90 per cent of what we say and do during a simulation.[16] As Paul Culleton further notes, "You have to create a vision based more on images and ideas and compelling pictures, as opposed to words."

Another vital element is the vision's evocative descriptors – statements that graphically embody the core values. Rather than merely articulating a desire or target, evocative descriptors help form a picture in the mind of the person hearing or seeing them. The vision statement of the fast food group McDonald's uses several evocative descriptors: *Our strategy is underpinned by our focus on running great restaurants, empowering our people, and getting faster, more innovative, and more efficient at solving problems for our customers and people.*[17]

When articulating vision descriptors, remember how the statement will be organized (structure, information flow) and how it will feel (the behaviour called for and the needs to be met). Judging by many corporations' bland vision statements, leaders often struggle to produce descriptions with enough detail. A powerful vision should form a gripping image in one's mind.

To be sure, leaders cannot communicate directly with each person in their company. This means they must learn to persuade from a distance. And by enlisting people who believe in what they're doing, they can cultivate buy-in and enthusiasm.

For this, leaders need to send the right signals through the company and personally live up to the change they're asking others to create. This goes beyond modelling behaviour; it means making day-to-day decisions that support the vision. A big part of this comes from putting enough resources behind the idea, not just in terms of capital investment, but allocating the right people to work on the vision and setting measurable targets to benchmark progress.

In addition, written strategies, compensation plans, measurement systems and annual budgets are powerful levers for influencing behaviour. They "push" people in the right direction by setting expectations and defining rewards and advancement. It therefore follows that the success of these tools relies upon authority, loyalty and the expectation of reward and progression. And the tools will be especially useful when realizing a vision requires improving company performance or reshaping its culture.

But leaders must also "pull" employees by defining an attractive future state so that individuals want to change for themselves. This will only happen if employees believe the new operating methods will better meet their needs than existing approaches – for example, by promising to create less frustration or reduce wasted energy, or through boosting the likelihood of advancement. "Pulling" takes different forms. At the lowest level, it requires active listening and the ability to give individual feedback in a way that strengthens relationships. At the team level, it means defining a personal vision and making it a common one to inspire a critical mass of people.

Push and pull approaches are complementary. Alone, neither approach will be enough to alter embedded habits or working practices to bring about change.[18] Most leaders tend to be adept at one or the other. To improve your capability to do both, you should strive to understand employee preferences and find ways to develop skills. You must also surround yourself with people who can supplement your communication abilities.

Involving the broader organization in your plans is important because you will otherwise invite unhelpful speculation. Company grapevines fill information voids, which can power the rumour mill and distort your message. Leaders must take control of the narrative before it gets away from them. It could be as simple as creating an in-house newsletter or writing a column in a corporate magazine to communicate the vision. Some leaders use vision boards to represent their goals visually. Typically, these are poster-sized and contain images and text that embody what you're trying to accomplish.

Freshly appointed CEOs often deliver speeches that set out their vision early on. On her first day as CEO of NatWest Group in 2019, Alison Rose shared her vision for the bank's future and explained what colleagues should expect. This included remaining curious and investing in new skills and capabilities to build a culture of continuous learning at the bank.[19] Technology has made corporate storytelling more immersive and engaging. Amanda Blanc, Group CEO at the insurer Aviva, releases regular videos alongside quarterly results that outline and reinforce her ambitions for the company, such as making improvements in delivery, a commitment to high performance and unwavering financial discipline. "We will win," said Blanc in 2020.[20] One final note is that leaders are much better able to influence people when they are respected, seen as trustworthy and believed to have sound judgement.[21]

The limitations of visioning and how to overcome them

One trap to avoid is creating a vision that key stakeholders view as grandiose or unrealistic. The fall from grace of Bombardier, the once-mighty Canadian aerospace company, is a cautionary tale. Bombardier started as a snowmobile manufacturer in the 1930s.[22] It set out its vision to become a substantial aircraft manufacturer in the 1990s as it sought to expand through acquisitions of the De Havilland division of Boeing and then Learjet. In 2005, Bombardier's long-time CEO Laurent Beaudoin placed a big bet on the C Series passenger aircraft programme to fuel the company's growth. Beaudoin's vision was to build Bombardier into a top-tier global aircraft manufacturer. In the process, however, the company took on a lot of debt, while the project suffered significant cost overruns and delays.[23]

The jets entered service in July 2016, 18 months late. However, Beaudoin's underestimation of the competitive response was the final nail in the coffin. The C Series was designed to compete with variants of Airbus's A320, and Airbus decided to reduce prices to meet the new aircraft head-to-head.[24] The result was poor sales, unsustainable losses and ultimately the need to let Airbus acquire the programme.[25] In 2017, Bombardier was forced to sell control of the C Series to Airbus for a token sum of $1; they relabelled the aircraft as the A220.[26] By 2020, Bombardier's then-CEO, Alain Bellemare, was ousted. The lesson is this: leaders must not overreach and commit to an unachievable vision. The ability to articulate a compelling vision with bold self-confidence is desirable, but what may initially seem visionary may turn out to be grandiose.

Reflection: Have you seen examples of leaders establishing unrealistic or grandiose visions? If so, what was the result?

Developing your visioning capabilities

You can become better at visioning – through intentional observation, imaginative visualization and clarification. One technique for developing visioning ability is the *architect's exercise*. Every time you enter a new home or office, take a few minutes to think about how you would change the space to make it a more attractive place to live or work. As you do this, write down observations and insights as the basis for reflection. Keeping a journal of thoughts can help capture insights and spark ideas for other concepts.

Another helpful process is organizing a "visioning workshop," where you and your team meet off-site to envision the enterprise's future collectively. In such workshops, the group uses pattern recognition (see Chapter 1) to anticipate the competitive, regulatory and financial landscapes the firm will face in the future. Then, perhaps through the systems analysis and scenario-planning discussed in Chapters 2 and 3, you can explore how the organization must frame and solve its most important problems as described in Chapter 4. Finally, you can work with the team to define the ambitious, achievable end state that you aspire to realize.

You do this by breaking up participants into small groups where each person describes the scene in their mind's eye. Each team member collates these images and presents them to the whole workshop. The process helps individual leaders clarify their thinking and provides a sense of what degree of change the top team might accept. This can help leaders shape a commonly held vision of the future while staying more in control of the visioning process. The downside is that visioning workshops involving just top leaders may not engage subordinates. Engaging others early on can help build commitment inside the organization, though some leaders may not wish to share a vision until it is fully formed.

Summary

Visioning is the process of creating a compelling vision for the future and using that vision to guide and motivate others to realize it. A vision is an inspiring picture of what the organization could become. It provides a sense of direction and purpose for the organization and its members. Visioning in leadership involves developing and communicating the vision through powerful simplification and storytelling that align the organization's strategies, policies and actions with the vision. The next chapter explores the sixth and final discipline of strategic thinking: *political savvy*.

Visioning Checklist

1. How important is it that you develop a shared vision for your organization?
2. Should you develop the vision using a "look forwards then reason back" approach, a "take stock and imagine possibilities" approach, or both?
3. How can you enhance your visioning capabilities, such as by regularly doing the architect's exercise?
4. How can you enhance your ability to communicate simply and powerfully?

To Learn More

Built to Last: Successful Habits of Visionary Companies by Jim Collins and Jerry I. Porras

Start with Why: How Great Leaders Inspire Everyone to Take Action by Simon Sinek and his TED Talk "How Great Leaders Inspire Action"

Chapter 6

THE DISCIPLINE OF POLITICAL SAVVY

POLITICAL SAVVY IS the ability to navigate and influence the political landscape of organizations. It involves understanding the underlying power dynamics, the motivations and interests of different stakeholders, and the potential implications of various courses of action. Political savvy is an essential element of strategic thinking for leaders of businesses, as it allows them to effectively navigate and manage political environments to achieve their goals and objectives. It is a combination of knowledge, skills and attitudes, and it requires a deep understanding of your organization, its resources and culture, and its political landscape.

The higher you go, the more political organizations become. This is partly because the people at the top are intelligent and ambitious. They have *agendas* – both in the business and in terms of recognition and advancement – that they aspire to advance. Further contributing to politicization at the top is the fact that the problems to be solved and decisions to be made at that level are more ambiguous. There seldom are "right" answers, so there is vigorous debate over the best way forward. The combination of ambitious people and ambiguous problems means that politics becomes a primary driver of outcomes at the highest levels of business. To develop and realize your goals, you must think strategically about building and sustaining alliances inside your organization.

In addition, you need to be proactive in shaping the external political environment in which your organization operates. This means establishing and managing critical relationships with customers, suppliers and other key players in the value chain, such as joint venture and alliance partners. It also means teaming up to influence the powerful institutions that shape the "rules of the game," including governments at multiple levels, non-governmental organizations, the media and investors.

In seeking to influence the rules of the game, it's helpful to imagine you are a *corporate diplomat.*[1] International diplomats seek to protect and advance the interests of their nations by fostering relationships, building alliances and negotiating agreements. As a corporate diplomat, you must learn to do the same to protect and promote the interests of your business.

To become more politically savvy, you must build your capacity to diagnose political systems and develop strategies that advance your strategic objectives, internally and externally. Your ability to do this rests, first and foremost, on your willingness to embrace politics and understand its fundamental logic. With that as a foundation, you must learn to assess the landscape and use your insights to craft strategies for influencing people. Those strategies include leveraging the "power of fair process" to bring people along with your ideas, discussed in Chapter 4, and recognizing the impact of compelling visions that "pull" people forwards, explored in Chapter 5.

Understanding and embracing politics

To understand the dangers of not embracing politics or misunderstanding its fundamental logic, consider the following example, which summarizes an actual situation. After just four months in her new job at Van Horn Foods, Alina Nowak (names have been changed) was deeply frustrated by the bureaucratic politics in the corporate headquarters. A successful sales and marketing professional, Nowak had risen through the country-management ranks of Van Horn, a leading international food company, to become the firm's managing director in her native Poland. She was a hard-driving, results-orientated executive who drove dramatic growth in her territory.

Based on this success, Nowak was assigned to turn around the company's struggling operations in the Balkans. She thrived in this complex multinational environment. Two and a half years later, the Balkans business was on track to achieve sustained double-digit growth. Accordingly, the senior leadership at Van Horn recognized Nowak's potential and decided she needed regional experience to prepare her for more senior roles. So, they appointed her as the regional vice president of marketing for Van Horn's operations across Europe, the Middle East and Africa (the EMEA region). In this new role, she oversaw the region's marketing strategy, branding and new-product development.

Van Horn had a matrix structure. Nowak reported directly to Marjorie Aaron, the senior vice president of corporate marketing, based at the company's US headquarters in Chicago. She also had a dotted-line reporting relationship with her former boss, Harald Eisenberg, the international vice president for EMEA operations, to whom all the country managing directors reported.

Nowak started her new role with enthusiasm, having one-on-one conversations with managing directors across the EMEA region and her former boss. Drawing upon those discussions and her own experiences in the field, Nowak concluded that the most pressing problem in the region was finding ways to better manage the tension between centralizing and decentralizing product-development decisions. Specifically, to what degree should the company require standard product formulations and packaging across the region, and to what degree should it allow some flexibility for local variations in taste?

Nowak put together a presentation outlining the results of her initial assessment and recommendations for improvements. Her proposal included increasing centralization in some areas (for example, decisions concerning overall brand identity and positioning) while giving the country managing directors more flexibility in others (such as making limited recipe adjustments). She then scheduled a virtual meeting with Aaron and Eisenberg, who listened attentively and seemed to see merits in her approach. They instructed her to consult with the stakeholders most affected by this organizational change – Van Horn's corporate product development and marketing executives in the US and the managing directors in the EMEA region.

Following Aaron's direction, she met virtually with David Wallace (the corporate senior vice president of product development), his staff, and Van Horn's corporate marketing team members. She then flew to Chicago to present to a group of some 30 people in the product development and marketing teams. They offered many suggestions, virtually all of which would result in more centralization of decision-making.

It also became clear to Nowak during the meeting – watching the body language and listening to the comments – that there were significant tensions between the corporate product development and marketing teams. "I've walked into a political minefield," she thought. She came away from the meeting with greater sympathy for her predecessor in the regional strategy role, with whom she'd had frequent clashes when she was a country managing director.

Her call with the EMEA managing directors – her old colleagues – also didn't go well. They were happy to accept Nowak's ideas for increased flexibility. But opposition hardened as soon as she mentioned any additional limits to their autonomy. One respected MD, Rolf Eiklid, said that getting more flexibility in the proposed areas wouldn't compensate for what they would be giving up. As country MDs had P&L responsibility for their territories and significant autonomy in allocating local resources, Nowak knew they could not be forced to accept the changes. She was left wondering whether she had the patience and finesse to navigate the politics of her new regional role.

Nowak's experience is a classic example of what happens when leaders reach positions where they can no longer rely on positional authority to get things done. To be successful, she needed to shift to thinking and manoeuvring politically and to lead through influence, not authority. The foundation for doing so is embracing the need to think about organizations through a political lens. Some leaders struggle with doing this. If you dislike politics, you must get over it. If it helps, think of what you are doing as building alliances to achieve important things.

What does it mean to think politically about organizations? The starting point is to visualize your business (and its external environment, too) as a collection of powerful actors pursuing their *agendas* – combinations of organizational and personal objectives they are trying to achieve. As discussed in Chapter 2, businesses are systems that have structures and processes that impact on what gets done. But, as mentioned above, the combination of ambitious people and ambiguous problems means that important decisions at the top (and externally) are often made because they are supported by *winning coalitions* of key decision-makers, or they are not made because there are *blocking coalitions* of opponents.[2]

To achieve your objectives, you need to identify potential winning coalitions – the people who collectively have the power to support your agenda – and think about how you will build those coalitions. Nowak needed approval from Aaron and Wallace on the corporate side and Eisenberg on the EMEA side. Together, they were the winning coalition that she needed to build.

Think too about potential blocking coalitions – those who collectively have the power to say no – and how you can avoid having opposition coalesce. Who might ally themselves to try to block your agenda, and why? How might they seek to oppose you? If you have insight into where opposition might come from, you can work to neutralize it. For Nowak, there were potential blocking coalitions in the corporate organization and among the regional MDs.

Recognize also that relationships and alliances are *not* the same thing. This is not to say that relationships aren't valuable; they certainly are. However, they are not the sole basis for building alliances because understanding people's agendas and your alignment with them – or lack thereof – is also essential. You can have a strong relationship with someone but have competing incentives. You can also have a neutral or even negative relationship with someone but be allies because your agendas align or because you can support each other to achieve complementary goals.

Defining your influence objectives

The first step in developing your influence is seeking clarity about *why* you need the support of others. Nowak's goal was to negotiate a new deal between her new and old bosses about the ways marketing decisions would be made in the EMEA region. The status quo reflected a long-standing compromise between the two sides. On the face of it, any changes were win–lose propositions for one side or the other. The implication was that an agreement, if one could be negotiated at all, would be a set of trades that both sides could support.

Reflection: Is there a substantial influence challenge you are facing? Is it helpful for you to think through it systematically? If so, take a few minutes to write a summary of it.

Understanding the key decision-makers

Armed with a clear understanding of *what* you're trying to accomplish, you can now focus on *whose* support is essential and *how* you will secure it. Start by identifying the alliances you need to build to achieve your objectives. To what extent do you need to gain the support of others over whom you don't have authority?

You may need to explore whether there are exchanges or "deals" you can strike that might help to win people over. Figure 15 summarizes common "currencies" for exchange in

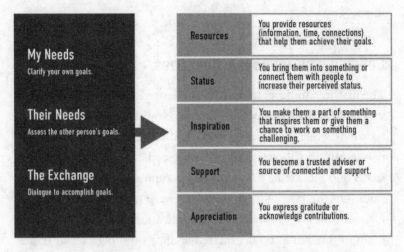

Figure 15: The common currencies for exchange in organizations organizations, including providing resource or inspiration, confirming higher status, giving personal support and even simply expressing appreciation. To do this well requires clarity, not just about your needs but what others see as valuable.

On top of identifying *potential exchanges*, you need to assess *situational pressures*, which means understanding the forces that are guiding the key decision-makers because of the context in which they operate. Think in terms of driving and restraining forces. Driving forces push people in the direction you want them to go, and restraining forces are situational reasons they would say no.[3] Social psychology research has shown that people overestimate the impact of personality and underestimate the impact of situational pressures in reaching conclusions about why people act the way they do.[4] Rolf's opposition to Nowak's proposal could be rooted in his inflexibility and a need to preserve his power and status, or he could be responding to situational pressures such as the need to achieve his business goals. So, take the time to think about the forces driving the people you want to influence. Then find ways to increase the drive and remove some restraints.

You will also need to focus on how the people you want to influence perceive their alternatives or choices. What are the options from which they believe they can choose? Critical to your *understanding of perceptions of alternatives* is the ability to work out whether opponents believe that overt or covert resistance can succeed in preserving the status quo. If so, it could be essential to convince them that the status quo is no longer a viable option. Once people believe that change will happen regardless of what they do, the game often shifts from outright opposition to a competition to influence what change will occur. Could Nowak have convinced the key decision-makers that the current situation was unacceptable, and that change needed to happen?

Concerns about the implementation of agreements also fall into this category. People may believe that others' concessions will not be honoured, and that they are better off fighting for the status quo than taking a chance on an alternative. If worries about *insecure contracts* are blocking progress, see whether there are ways to increase confidence levels. For example, you might propose phasing in the changes, with each step linked to success in implementing the previous ones.

Reflection: Use the table on the next page to assess potential exchanges to win over key decision-makers. Also, assess the situational pressures driving them, and their perceptions of the alternative choices they believe they have.

Key Decision-makers	Potential Exchanges	Situational Pressures	Alternatives

Mapping influence networks

Decision-makers are usually influenced by the opinions of those on whom they rely for advice. So, take the time to map *influence networks*. Ask yourself: Who influences whom on the issues at hand? Influence networks can play a substantial role in determining whether you achieve your objectives. Decision-makers often defer to others whose opinions they trust regarding important issues and decisions.

Influence networks are channels for communication and persuasion that operate in parallel with the formal structure – a sort of shadow organization.[5] How do you map influence networks? A simple way is to use the "bullseye" diagram shown in Figure 16, using Nowak's example to illustrate how it works. Start by identifying the key decision-makers and put them in the middle. Then identify other people or groups who influence the decision-makers and place them in circles further out. The further from the centre they are, the less influence these individuals or groups have. Use

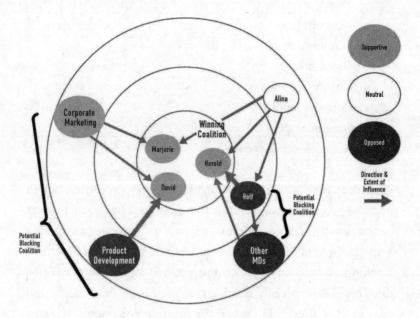

Figure 16: Mapping influence networks

arrows to indicate the direction and strength of influence, with thicker arrows indicating more influence. Then assess who you believe to be supportive, neutral and opposed. Finally, identify potential winning and blocking coalitions.

Reflection: For the influence challenge you are facing, would it be valuable to identify key decision-makers and map influence networks?

Crafting your influence strategies

Armed with deeper insight into the people you need to sway, you can develop your influence strategies by leveraging these seven "tools":

- Consultation
- Framing
- Social pressure
- Choice-shaping
- Entanglement
- Sequencing
- Action-forcing events

Consultation is an influence technique that promotes buy-in because people feel invested in the outcome. Being effective at consultation means you must engage in active listening. Jeff Immelt, General Electric's former chief executive, has described listening as "the single most undervalued and underdeveloped business skill, especially in an age of increasing uncertainty and fast-paced change."[6] However, the more senior leaders become, the less they typically listen. And subordinates may be reluctant to tell you what you don't want to hear. You can overcome this by seeking input and incorporating feedback into your approach. Good consultation starts with posing focused, genuine questions and encouraging people to voice their real concerns. Then you summarize and feedback what you've heard.

This approach signals that you're paying attention and taking the conversation seriously. The power of active listening as an influence strategy is vastly underrated. It can promote acceptance of difficult decisions, channel people's thinking and help you frame choices in productive ways. Because the questions leaders ask and how they summarize responses have a powerful effect on people's perceptions, active listening and framing are impactful persuasive techniques. See the table opposite for additional advice on how to listen actively.

Be Present

Give the person your complete and undivided attention.

- Focus your complete attention only on the other person; turn away from your computer and ignore your phone.
- Make direct eye contact.
- Avoid looking around at other people or things.
- Paraphrase what you heard, using your own words, for example "what I heard is . . ."
- If needed, clarify your understanding of what was said, for example "If I understand you correctly you are saying . . ."

Encourage

Encourage the person to tell you what is on his/her mind.

- Verbally acknowledge with minimal interruptions: "Uh huh", "Mmm", "Yes"
- Nod your head to indicate you are listening.
- Lean towards the person.
- Listen without interrupting, suspend your judgement, and don't impose your solutions.
- Acknowledge and empathize with the person's feelings, for example "You seem to be feeling . . ."

Question

Learn from the conversation instead of confirming your exising beliefs.

- Pose questions that require a reflective response; avoid questions that require a yes/no answer.
- Use "Tell me more about that" to elicit more detail.
- Use "Why do you think that is the case?" to probe understanding of causes and effects.
- Use "What would happen if . . .?" and "What would happen then?" to expand thinking about consequences.

Summarize

Summarize what you heard and what agreements you have made.

- Begin with a concluding statement, "To summarize our discussion . . ."
- Include the most important facts, information, and agreements made during the conversation.
- Check that the other person has the same understanding as you do. "So, does that sound OK to you?"
- Thank the other person for the conversation.

Framing means using argument and analogy to articulate your definition of the problem to be solved and the set of acceptable solutions. It means carefully crafting your persuasive arguments on a person-by-person basis. Your messages should take an appropriate tone, tap into the motivations and agendas of the people you seek to influence and critically shape how the key players perceive their alternatives.

Nowak, for example, should have explored what it would take to move the MD Eiklid from being opposed to at least being neutral and, ideally, supportive. Did he have specific concerns that she could have addressed? Was there a set of trades that Eiklid would have found attractive if their implementation was guaranteed? Were there ways of helping him advance other agendas he cared about in exchange for his support of Nowak's approach?

As you frame your arguments, remember Aristotle's rhetorical categories of *logos*, *ethos* and *pathos*.[7] *Logos* is about making logical arguments – using data, facts and reasoned rationales to build your case for change. *Ethos* is about elevating the principles that should be applied (such as fairness) and the values that must be upheld (such as a culture of teamwork) in making decisions. *Pathos* is about fostering emotional connections with the people you seek to influence – for example, communicating an inspiring vision of what could be accomplished.

Framing usually means communicating a few key arguments, which are repeated until they sink in. This is similar in spirit to the idea of powerful simplification discussed in Chapter 5. Repetition is effective because people learn best through repeated reinforcement. By the third or fourth time we hear a song, we can't get it out of our minds. It is possible, though, to listen to a song so much that we get sick of it. Similarly, using the same words repeatedly makes it apparent that you're trying to persuade, which can provoke a backlash. The art of effective communication is to repeat and elaborate core themes without sounding like a parrot.

As you frame your arguments, think about how you can "inoculate" people against the counter-arguments you expect your opponents will make. Presenting and decisively refuting weak rebuttals immunizes audiences against the same arguments when they're in more potent forms. The table below provides a simple checklist for framing the arguments you need to make. Use the following categories and questions to identify how best to convince people.

Logos – data and reasoned arguments	• What data or analysis might they find persuasive? • What logic might appeal to them?
Ethos – principles, policies, and other "rules"	• Are there principles or policies that they could be convinced should operate here? • If you ask them to act counter to a principle or policy, can you help them justify making an exception?
Pathos – emotions, and meaning	• Are there emotional "triggers", for example, loyalty or contribution to the common good, to which you could appeal? • Can you help them create a sense of meaning by supporting or opposing a cause? • If they are overreacting emotionally, can you help them step back and get perspective?

Social pressure is the persuasive impact of the opinions of others and the norms of the societies and identity groups that they are part of. Knowing that a highly respected person already supports a decision alters others' assessment of its attractiveness. So convincing opinion leaders to make commitments of support and to mobilize their networks can give you a powerful leveraging effect.

Research by social psychologists including Robert B. Cialdini, author of *Influence: The Psychology of Persuasion*, suggest that people prefer to behave in the following ways:[8]

- *Remain consistent with firmly held values and beliefs*: People tend to share values with the groups they identify with. They are virtually certain to resist if you ask them to engage in behaviour inconsistent with these values. As James Clear, author of the article "Why Facts Don't Change Our Minds" notes, trying to get people to change things that are deeply connected to their sense of identity is unlikely to take you far.[9]
- *Remain consistent with prior commitments and decisions*: Failure to honour commitments tends to incur social sanctions, and inconsistency signals unreliability and damages reputations. People prefer not to make choices that require them to reverse prior commitments or set undesirable precedents.
- *Repay obligations*: Reciprocity is a strong social norm, and people are vulnerable to appeals for support that invoke past favours they've received from you and others.
- *Preserve reputations*: Choices that preserve or enhance one's reputation are viewed favourably, whereas those that could jeopardize one's reputation are viewed negatively.

The implication is that you need to avoid, as far as possible, asking others to do things that are inconsistent with their identities and prior commitments, decrease their status, threaten their reputations, or risk evoking the disapproval of respected others. Remember that if someone you need to influence has a competing prior commitment, you should look for ways to help them gracefully escape from it.

Choice-shaping is about influencing how people perceive their alternatives. How can you make it hard for them to say no. Or, as Roger Fisher, co-author of *Getting to Yes*, put it, always try to offer "yesable propositions."[10] Sometimes it is best to frame choices broadly, and at other times more narrowly. If you're asking someone to support something that could be seen as setting an undesirable precedent, it might best be framed as an isolated situation, independent of other decisions. In other cases, it could be better for you to frame things in terms of connections to more significant concerns.

It's tough to sell people on choices they see as win–lose propositions. Broadening the range of issues or options can facilitate mutually beneficial trades that enlarge the pie. Progress, likewise, can be stalled by the presence of toxic, irreconcilable issues. These can sometimes be neutralized by setting them aside for future consideration or by making up-front commitments that allay anxieties.

Entanglement is the idea that by progressing step by step, you can get people to go to places they wouldn't go in a single leap. Mapping out a progressive pathway from A to B is an effective influence strategy because each small step creates a new baseline for people to decide whether to take the next one. Getting people involved in the shared diagnosis of organizational problems can be a form of entanglement. If you involve key people early in diagnosing issues, it makes it difficult for them to avoid having to make tough decisions later on. Once there is consensus on the problem, you can shift to defining the options and then to the criteria used to evaluate them. By the end of such a process, people are often willing to accept outcomes they would never have agreed to at the outset.

Because entanglement can have a powerful impact, it's essential to influence decision-making before momentum builds in the wrong direction. You can gain influence in organizations by taking the initiative to surface and frame problems. As already mentioned, decision-making processes in organizations are like rivers: big decisions are powerfully shaped by earlier processes that define the problem, identify alternatives and establish criteria for evaluating costs and benefits. By the time the problem and the options have been defined, the river is already flowing powerfully and cutting a channel to a particular outcome.

Sequencing means being strategic about the order in which you influence people to build momentum in desired directions, as we explored in Chapter 3.[11] If you approach the right people first, you can set a virtuous cycle of alliance-building in motion. Success in gaining one respected ally makes it easier to recruit others – and your resource base increases. With broader support, the likelihood increases that your agenda will succeed, making it easier to recruit more supporters. Based on her assessment of influence patterns at Van Horn, for example, Nowak should have met first with key people in corporate marketing and then with product development VP David Wallace to try to secure his support.

More generally, Nowak's sequencing plan should have consisted of a well-thought-through series of one-on-one and group meetings to create momentum for a new deal. The critical point here is getting the mix right. One-on-one meetings are effective for getting the lie of the land – for instance, hearing people's positions, shaping their views by providing new or extra information, or potentially negotiating side deals. But the participants in a serious negotiation often aren't willing to make their final concessions and commitments unless they're sitting face-to-face with others. That is when group meetings are particularly effective.

Action-forcing events are approaches that get people to stop deferring decisions, delaying and avoiding the commitment of scarce resources.[12] When your success requires the coordinated action of many people, delay by a single individual can have a cascade effect, giving others an excuse not to proceed. You must therefore eliminate inaction as an option. You do this by setting up action-forcing events that induce people to commit or act. Meetings, review sessions, teleconferences and deadlines can all help create and sustain momentum and increase the psychological pressure to follow through.

Reflection: For the influence challenge you have been analyzing, can you leverage the seven strategies of consultation, framing, social pressure, choice-shaping, entanglement, sequencing and action-forcing events to achieve your objectives?

The importance of emotional intelligence

Your ability to influence rests in no small part on your emotional intelligence: the capability to see beyond our objectives and perspectives. It allows us to put ourselves in other people's shoes. Leaders with higher emotional intelligence are better at "reading" other people's emotions, which is the foundation for effective social influence. This can be enhanced by reading other people's body language, catching the mood of the room and practising the art of active listening. That means consciously understanding the meaning conveyed in words rather than just passively hearing them.

Self-awareness will help you to manage your behaviours and emotions. You can boost your levels of self-awareness by observing how your feelings have a ripple effect and can impact on others, as well as knowing what and who does things that spur an emotional reaction of anger, irritation or exasperation in oneself.

A powerful way to develop your emotional intelligence is through an exercise called "perceptual positions."[13] Doing so means self-consciously adopting perspectives other than your own in challenging situations. Of course, it's natural to look at the world through the lens of your interests and aspirations. However, this also means that you may have blind spots or biases that prevent you from perceiving the real issue or identifying more constructive ways to engage and solve a problem.

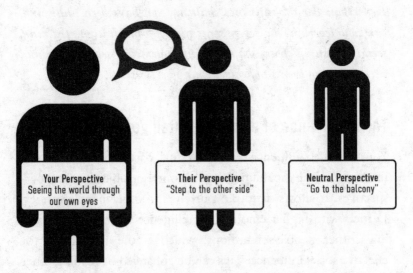

Figure 17: Perceptual positions

The first approach is to strive to see the situation through the eyes of the other person or people who are involved. Do your best to look at it as you imagine they would. As you do that, remember that empathy is not the same as sympathy. Understanding another's perspective doesn't mean you need to give up on what you are trying to do. But it rarely hurts to have a deeper understanding.

The second approach is to take a neutral, dispassionate view of what is happening. Ask yourself: What would someone with no history or explicit interest in the situation think and observe about what is going on? What advice would they give you about how to handle this situation?

The goal of this exercise is to become fluid in shifting between the three perspectives. Start with how you see the situation. Then step to the other side and see if it offers new insights or perspectives. Then go to the balcony, look at the problem from a neutral perspective, and see if it reveals new or different aspects. Finally, come back to your perspective and explore whether your thinking about the situation has changed. Practised with diligence, the perceptual positions exercise will enhance your emotional intelligence and hence your ability to leverage it and influence others.

Developing your political savvy

You can develop your political savvy by focusing intentionally on seeing the world through a political lens. Take time to observe and analyze the political landscape of your organization and its external environment. Start by assessing who has influence. What are their agendas and sources of power? Do they have deep technical expertise or access to information? Or is it based on access to key decision-makers or alliances with other influential players?

Then, experiment with employing the influence tools discussed previously, such as framing, choice-shaping and sequencing. Ask how you can best frame your arguments to appeal to the influential players' interests. How would you like them to perceive their alternatives? What is the best order in which to talk to people to create momentum?

Finally, work on building your networks. Political savvy often involves building and leveraging a network of relationships, within your organization or externally. Investing in developing and strengthening your networking skills, and building a diverse and strategic network of contacts, can help you become more influential.

Summary

Political savvy helps you to navigate and influence the political landscape of organizations. By understanding the underlying power dynamics, the agendas of different stakeholders and patterns of influence, you can better formulate strategies to build alliances in support of your goals. There are many tools for exerting influence in organizations, including consultation, framing, social pressure and sequencing.

Political Savvy Checklist

1. What are the most important alliances you need to build – both within your organization and externally – to advance your agenda?

2. What agendas are the other influential players pursuing? Where might their agenda align with yours, and where might it conflict?

3. How does influence work in the organization? Who defers to whom on key issues of concern?

4. What are the motivations of pivotal people, the situational pressures driving them and their perceptions of their choices?

5. What are the elements of an effective influence strategy? How should you frame your arguments? Might influence tools such as entanglement, sequencing and action-forcing events help?

To Learn More

Influence: The Psychology of Persuasion by Robert B. Cialdini

Getting to Yes: Negotiating an Agreement Without Giving In by Roger Fisher, William Ury and Bruce Patton

Getting Past No: Negotiating with Difficult People by William Ury

7 Rules of Power: Surprising – but True – Advice on How to Get Things Done and Advance Your Career by Jeffrey Pfeffer

DEVELOPING YOUR STRATEGIC-THINKING ABILITY

IN THE INTRODUCTION, I summarized the strategic-thinking capacity (STC) of business leaders using the following equation:

STC = Endowment + Experience + Exercise

Your *endowment* is built by your genetics and upbringing. *Experience* is your involvement in situations that develop your strategic-thinking ability, ideally ones where you can demonstrate your abilities to more senior leaders. *Exercise* is the mental work you do to build your strategic-thinking muscles.

By definition, there's nothing to be done concerning your endowment as a strategic thinker. The key, then, is to focus on how to get better, regardless of your starting point. Doing so means gaining experience and exercising your brain.

Gaining experience (and exposure)

"It's not who you know, it's who knows you" is a basic tenet of network-building. It's also a core part of strategic thinking. It's not enough to be a strong strategic thinker; the people who influence your career trajectory – your boss, other senior leaders, the HR and talent-development executives – need to see you have the ability and potential.

Many leaders struggle with this because they don't get opportunities to demonstrate strategic-thinking skills. To increase your visibility, you should do the following, regardless of what role you are in:[1]

- *Show you see the big picture*: Help others see that you have a deep understanding of your organization's context and challenges. Take advantage of opportunities to link discussions of current issues to the bigger picture.
- *Demonstrate you are a critical thinker*: Strive always to ground your arguments in solid analysis and show how you reached your conclusions. In both written and verbal modes, seek to communicate concisely and logically.
- *Have a point of view*: Before every interaction where strategic issues could be discussed, take the time to review the key topics and analyses. Think about the specific insights you could contribute or questions you could ask.
- *Highlight your ability to observe trends and envision potential futures*: Help others see that you are tuned in to relevant trends. Show that you can look beyond the now to foresee how the future could unfold.

- *Speak like a strategic thinker*: Use words and phrases that highlight your strategic-thinking ability, such as "strategic goals," "root causes" and "competitive responses."
- *Engage in constructive challenge*: Ask the hard questions without being disruptive or disrespectful. Show that you don't take things at face value and can think a few "moves" out to probe how things are likely to evolve.
- *Don't rehash problems; reframe them*: Identify new ways to define the problem and the potential solutions. Be alert to opportunities to demonstrate you have the mental flexibility to see things from multiple perspectives.

Exercising your brain

In the Introduction, I defined strategic thinking as "the set of mental disciplines leaders use to recognize potential threats and opportunities, establish priorities to focus attention, and mobilize themselves and their organizations to envision and enact promising paths forward." I also identified six mental disciplines that collectively lay the foundation of strategic thinking: pattern recognition, systems analysis, mental agility, structured problem-solving, visioning and political savvy.

It is possible to boost your brainpower to develop the six disciplines. This is due to *neuroplasticity*. Until the late 1990s, scientists believed human brains remained relatively static after early childhood. But subsequent research demonstrated the brain's miraculous ability to continuously forge and re-form the neural pathways and connections that process information, provided it is stimulated in specific ways.[2] The implication for developing strategic-thinking ability is that you can expect to get better if you discipline yourself to do the right mental exercises. These exercises are summarized below for each of the six disciplines. Build your own strategic-thinking training plan by doing combinations of these exercises on a regular basis.

Developing the discipline of pattern recognition

Pattern recognition is the ability of the human brain to identify and detect regularities or patterns in the world around us. In business, pattern recognition is your ability to observe the complex, uncertain, volatile, ambiguous domains in which your business operates and identify potential threats and opportunities.

To develop your pattern-recognition abilities, focus on doing the following:

- *Learning about the underlying mechanisms*: Knowing the underlying principles and mechanisms of human pattern recognition can help you understand how your brain processes and recognizes patterns. It will provide you with strategies for improving your pattern-recognition skills.
- *Immersing yourself*: Your pattern-recognition ability will improve if you devote yourself to learning about specific domains of interest. Try to discern the key variables that drive change and recognize trends in those domains. Cultivate your curiosity about why things work the way they do.
- *Engaging with experts*: Seek out people who already deeply understand domains of interest to you. Ask them to help you understand how they separate signal from noise and identity the most important patterns.

Developing the discipline of systems analysis

Systems analysis is about building simplified mental models of complex domains. It focuses on the connections and interactions between the elements of a system rather than on the individual components in isolation.

To develop your systems-analysis abilities, focus on the following:

- *Understanding the principles of systems analysis*: To think effectively about complex systems, it helps to have a good understanding of the underlying concepts and how they are applied. You can learn about this by reading books and articles, attending workshops or training programmes and working with experienced systems thinkers.
- *Practising analyzing and thinking about systems*: Like many other skills, systems-thinking improves with practice. The more you practise seeing the world in terms of systems, the better you will become at it. This can involve applying systems-thinking to real-world problems or working on case studies and simulations.

Developing the discipline of mental agility

Mental agility lets you look at situations from multiple perspectives, think through potential scenarios and anticipate actions and reactions. It enables you to look beyond the present situation and consider the long-term implications of different courses of action.

You can develop your mental agility by:

- *Practising level-shifting*: Be intentional about shifting your perspective from the big picture to the fine details and back again. If you find yourself stuck on the ground, try to elevate your viewpoint. If you are stuck in the clouds, discipline yourself to return to earth.
- *Engaging in activities that develop your game-playing ability*: Many activities and games can help to improve your mental agility, such as chess, puzzles and brain teasers. These activities can help improve your ability to think about moves and countermoves.

Developing the discipline of structured problem-solving

Structured problem-solving breaks the process of analyzing problems down into discrete steps, such as identifying key stakeholders, framing the problem, generating potential solutions, evaluating and selecting the best course of action, and implementing the solution.

Take these steps to develop your structured-problem-solving ability:

- *Understand the principles of structured problem-solving*: To get better at structured problem-solving, it's essential to understand the basic principles, such as the steps in the process, the tools and techniques used in each step and the common pitfalls and challenges.
- *Practise structured problem-solving*: As with the other strategic-thinking disciplines, structured problem-solving improves with application. The more you practise structured problem-solving, the better you will become at it.

This can involve working on a variety of problems and seeking feedback and guidance from others.

Developing the discipline of visioning

Visioning is the process of creating a compelling and inspiring vision for an organization's future and communicating that vision to guide and motivate others. A vision is a clear, inspiring picture of what the organization could become. It helps to provide a sense of direction and purpose for the organization and its members.

You can boost visioning abilities through:

- *Understanding the principles of effective visioning*: To be good at visioning, you need a solid understanding of the underlying principles, such as the role of vision in leadership, the characteristics of a compelling vision and the process of developing and communicating a vision through powerful simplification.
- *Practising microvisioning*: Find small examples of problems, issues or situations where you can practise your visioning skills. When you see such opportunities, think about what you could do to improve things substantially. For example, use the architect's exercise described in Chapter 5 to imagine how a room or home could be set up differently.

Developing the discipline of political savvy

Political savvy is the ability to navigate and influence your organization's internal and external political landscapes. To do so, you must understand the motivations and interests of different stakeholders, map networks of relationships and craft influence strategies by:

- *Observing and analyzing political landscapes*: Look at your organization or its external environment through a political lens. Focus on identifying stakeholders and assessing their agendas and interests.
- *Seeking to understand the dynamics of power and influence*: Look for patterns in who has power and why they have it, as well as who influences whom and why.

Beyond advice on the six disciplines, there are some more general habits you can work on to enhance your strategic-thinking ability:

- *Reflecting and assessing your thinking*: Take time to regularly reflect on your progress and evaluate where you are doing well and where you need to improve. This can help you to identify where to focus, so you continue to develop as a strategic thinker.
- *Seeking feedback and advice*: To become a better strategic thinker, be systematic in seeking input from others, such as mentors, peers or experts. They can provide valuable perspectives and insights that can help to improve your strategic-thinking skills.

Building a strategic-thinking team

Throughout the book, I have focused on developing the strategic-thinking capability of individual business leaders like you. The reality, though, is that much strategic thinking in business happens in teams. It is therefore essential to focus on how you can develop your team's capacity to think strategically.

To do that, first help your team understand what strategic thinking is and isn't. Then, focus collectively on how you approach the recognize–prioritize–mobilize cycle (Figure 1), assessing both how effective you are and how to decrease your cycle time.

Then introduce the six disciplines and explore, perhaps in separate sessions, what each one is, why it is important and how to develop it. At the risk of being self-serving, a good way to do this is to have your team members read and discuss chapters of this book with you.

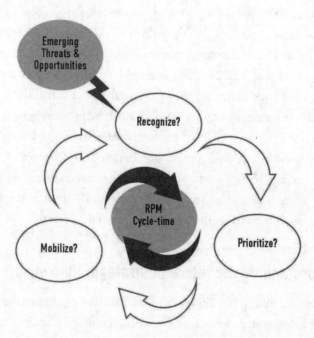

Figure 1: The recognize–prioritize–mobilize cycle

Beyond that, there is much you can do to develop the strategic-thinking capacity of your team by adopting these strategies:

- *Encourage a culture of strategic thinking*: Focus on creating a culture that values and encourages strategic thinking by role-modelling, recognizing and rewarding strategic thinking among your team members.
- *Provide development opportunities*: Explore whether you can provide training and development opportunities for team members to improve their strategic-thinking skills. This could include workshops, seminars, mentoring programmes and opportunities to learn from experts in the field.
- *Foster collaboration*: You can encourage team members to share ideas to expand their perspectives and build their pattern-recognition skills. You could devote some time to this in regular team meetings and provide opportunities for team members to work on specific projects together.
- *Invest in action learning*: You can foster learning by providing resources and support for team members to test new ideas and solve problems in a structured way, perhaps using the approaches detailed in Chapter 4. You could also provide a budget for experimentation, dedicated time for innovation and opportunities for team members to learn from failures and successes.

Understanding the future of strategic thinking

Strategic thinking has always been an essential capability for business leaders, but it will likely become even more important. The reason is that the business environment is becoming increasingly complex, uncertain, volatile and ambiguous. In this high-CUVA environment, your ability to think strategically will give your organization a durable competitive advantage.

Developing your strategic-thinking skills will help you anticipate and respond effectively to changes in the external environment, such as technological advancements, shifting market conditions and new competition. It will also help you understand your organization's strengths and weaknesses, allocate resources, prioritize initiatives and make trade-offs more effectively.

Furthermore, strategic thinking will help you deal with the increasing importance of innovation. You need to think strategically about how to innovate and create new products, services and business models that can help your business stay competitive. To succeed, you must be able to think creatively and be willing to take calculated risks.

Another factor that will make strategic thinking more vital is the growing importance of data and analytics. You will need to think strategically about collecting, analyzing and using data to make informed decisions. This will require you to think critically and analytically, and to be comfortable working with data and AI-enabled tools.

Finally, strategic thinking will be increasingly important as the world continues to become more interconnected. You will need to think strategically about navigating the complexities of the global business environment and building and maintaining relationships with key partners and stakeholders.

NOTES

Introduction: The Power of Strategic Thinking

1 Samantha Liss, "Advocate Aurora, Atrium Health to merge, creating $27B system", *Healthcare Dive*, 11 May 2022.

2 Robert Kabacoff, "Develop Strategic Thinkers Throughout Your Organization", *Harvard Business Review*, 7 February 2014.

3 Zenger Folkman, "Developing Strategic Thinking Skills: The Pathway to the Top", zengerfolkman.com/articles/developing-strategic-thinking-skills-the-pathway-to-the-top/, 8 February 2021.

4 Tom and David Kelley, *Creative Confidence: Unleashing the Creative Potential Within Us All*, Currency, 2013.

5 Nigel Cross, *Design Thinking: Understanding How Designers Think and Work*, Bloomsbury Visual Arts, second edition, 2023.

6 Warren Bennis and Burt Nanus, *Leaders: The Strategies for Taking Charge*, HarperBusiness, 2004. For an account of the history of its adoption and elaboration by the US Army, see "Who first originated the term VUCA (Volatility, Uncertainty, Complexity and Ambiguity)?", U.S. Army Heritage and Education Center, usawc.libanswers.com/faq/84869. For a more recent discussion of the implications for business, see Nate Bennett and G. James Lemoine, "What VUCA Really Means for You", *Harvard Business Review*, January–February 2014.

7 C. Basu, "The Importance of Porter's Diamond & Porter's Five Forces in Business", *Houston Chronicle*, 30 August 2021.

8 D. L. Costill, W. J. Fink and M. L. Pollock, "Muscle fiber composition and enzyme activities of elite distance runners", *Medicine & Science in Sports & Exercise*, Volume 8, Issue 2, summer 1976.

Chapter 1: The Discipline of Pattern Recognition

1 Arthur van de Oudeweetering, *Improve Your Chess Pattern Recognition*, New in Chess, 2014.

2   D. Silver, J. Schrittwieser, K. Simonyan et al., "Mastering the game of Go without human knowledge", *Nature*, Volume 550, 2017.

3   See Jon Russell, "Google's AlphaGo AI wins three-match series against the world's best Go player", *TechCrunch*, 25 May 2017.

4   Jack Welch commenting on shipping magnate Cornelius Vanderbilt's decision to invest in railways, Episode 1 – "A New War Begins" – of the 2012 History Channel mini-series The Men Who Built America.

5   See Srini Pillay, "Your Brain Can Only Take So Much Focus", *Harvard Business Review*, 12 May 2017.

6   Daniel Kahneman, "Of 2 Minds: How Fast and Slow Thinking Shape Perception and Choice [Excerpt]", *Scientific American*, 15 June 2012.

7   See "Bet You Didn't Notice 'The Invisible Gorilla'", *NPR*, 19 May 2010.

8   Nassim Nicholas Taleb, *The Black Swan: The Impact of the Highly Improbable*, Random House, 2007.

9   See Daniel Kahneman, *Thinking, Fast and Slow*, Farrar, Straus and Giroux, 2011.

10 Phil Rosenzweig, *The Halo Effect . . . and the Eight Other Business Delusions That Deceive Managers*, Free Press, 2007.

11 Ronak Patel, R. Nathan Spreng and Gary R. Turner, "Functional brain changes following cognitive and motor skills training: a quantitative meta-analysis" *Neurorehabilitation and Neural Repair*, Volume 27, Issue 3, March–April 2013.

12 Todd B. Kashdan, Ryne A. Sherman, Jessica Yarbro and David C. Funder, "How are curious people viewed and how do they behave in social situations? From the perspectives of self, friends, parents, and unacquainted observers", *Journal of Personality*, Volume 81, Issue 2, April 2013.

13 "Federal Express's Fred Smith on Innovation (1986 Interview)", *Inc.*, 1 October 1986.

14 Lesley Bartlett and Frances Vavrus, "Comparative Case Studies", *Educação & Realidade*, Volume 42, Issue 3, July 2017.

15 Gary Klein, "Developing Expertise in Decision Making", *Thinking & Reasoning*, Volume 3, Issue 4, 1997.

Chapter 2: The Discipline of Systems Analysis

1   Nicholas G. Heavens, Daniel S. Ward and Natalie M. Mahowald, "Studying and Projecting Climate Change with Earth System Models", *Nature Education Knowledge*, Volume 4(5), Issue 4, 2013.

2   See Mary-Ann Russon, "The cost of the Suez Canal blockage", BBC News, 29 March 2021, bbc.co.uk/news/business-56559073.

3 Edward Segal, "Blocked Suez Canal Is Latest Reminder Why Companies Need Crisis Plans", *Forbes*, 27 March 2021.

4 "Cascading failure", Wikimedia Foundation, accessed 22 July 2022, https://en.wikipedia.org/wiki/Cascading_failure.

5 Mark DeCambre, "Hedge-fund investor who made $2.6 billion on pandemic trades says omicron could be bullish for stock market", *MarketWatch*, 29 November 2021.

6 Jay R. Galbraith, *Designing Organizations: An Executive Guide to Strategy, Structure, and Process*, Jossey-Bass, 2001.

7 Tom Peters, "A Brief History of the 7-S ('McKinsey 7-S') Model", tompeters.com/2011/03/a-brief-history-of-the-7-s-mckinsey-7-s-model/

8 Peter M. Senge, *The Fifth Discipline: The Art & Practice of the Learning Organization*, Doubleday Business, 1990.

9 Eliyahu M. Goldratt and Jeff Cox, *The Goal: A Process of Ongoing Improvement*, 30th Anniversary Edition, North River Press, 2012.

10 See Mia Rabson, "From science to syringe: COVID-19 vaccines are miracles of science and supply chains", *Toronto Star*, 27 February 2021.

11 Amit S. Mukherjee, *Leading in the Digital World: How to Foster Creativity, Collaboration, and Inclusivity (Management on the Cutting Edge)*, The MIT Press, 2020.

12 Michael D. Watkins, "Assessing Your Organization's Crisis Response Plans", Harvard Business School Background Note 902-064, September 2001.

13 U.S. Army Center for Army Lessons Learned, www.army.mil/CALL.

14 See Steven Schuster, *The Art of Thinking in Systems: A Crash Course in Logic, Critical Thinking and Analysis-Based Decision Making*, independently published, 2021.

15 Kristina M. Gillmeister, "Development of Early Conceptions in Systems Thinking in an Environmental Context: An Exploratory Study of Preschool Students' Understanding of Stocks & Flows, Behavior Over Time and Feedback", PhD diss., State University of New York at Buffalo, 2017, Publication Number: AAT 10256359; Source: *Dissertation Abstracts International*, Volume: 78-11(E), Section: A, 2017.

Chapter 3: The Discipline of Mental Agility

1 For full quote see Jonathan Wai, "Seven Ways to Be More Curious", *Psychology Today*, 31 July 2014.

2 "First-move advantage in chess", Wikimedia Foundation, accessed 14 September 2022, en.wikipedia.org/wiki/First-move_advantage_in_chess.

3 "Game Theory – First Mover Advantage", Economics: Study Notes, Tutor2u.net, accessed October 2022, www.tutor2u.net/economics/reference/game-theory-first-mover-advantage.

4 In 1994, American mathematician John Forbes Nash, Jr. won a Nobel Prize for developing the concept of Nash equilibrium in game theory.

5 "Extensive-form game", Wikimedia Foundation, accessed 5 October 2021, en.wikipedia.org/wiki/Extensive-form_game.

6 Steven D. Levitt, John A. List and Sally E. Sadoff, "Checkmate: Exploring Backward Induction among Chess Players", *American Economic Review*, Volume 101, Issue 2, April 2011.

7 George Wright and George Cairns, *Scenario Thinking: Practical Approaches to the Future*, Palgrave Macmillan, 2011.

Chapter 4: The Discipline of Structured Problem-solving

1 This is an adaptation of the well-known RACI (Responsible, Accountable, Consulted, Informed) matrix, original versions of which were used for project management in the 1950s. For an overview of the methodology, see Bob Kantor, "The RACI matrix: Your blueprint for project success", CIO, 14 September 2022, www.cio.com/article/287088/project-management-how-to-design-a-successful-raci-project-plan.html.

2 The idea of fair process is rooted in thinking about procedural justice in the law. For an overview, see "Procedural justice", Wikimedia Foundation, accessed 14 April 2022, en.wikipedia.org/wiki/Procedural_justice. For an example of applying the concept to leadership, see W. Chan Kim and Renée Mauborgne, "Fair Process: Managing in the Knowledge Economy", *Harvard Business Review*, January 2003.

3 Albert Einstein and Leopold Infeld, *The Evolution of Physics*, Cambridge University Press, 1938.

4 Arnaud Chevallier and Albrecht Enders, *Solvable: A Simple Solution to Complex Problems*, FT Publishing International, 2022.

5 ibid.

6 Amos Tversky and Daniel Kahneman, "Loss Aversion in Riskless Choice: A Reference-Dependent Model", *The Quarterly Journal of Economics*, Volume 106, Issue 4, November 1991.

7 Michael A. Roberto, *Unlocking Creativity: How to Solve Any Problem and Make the Best Decisions by Shifting Creative Mindsets*, Wiley, 2019.

8 Graham Wallas, *The Art of Thought*, Harcourt, Brace and Company, 1926.

9 Daniel Ames, Richard Larrick and Michael Morris, "Scoring a Deal: Valuing Outcomes in Multi-Issue Negotiations", Columbia CaseWorks: Columbia Business School, spring 2012.

Chapter 5: The Discipline of Visioning

1 For an introduction to the process of visioning see Chapter 11 of Senge, *The Fifth Discipline*.

2 Christopher K. Bart, "Sex, lie, and mission statements", *Business Horizons*, Volume 40, Issue 6, November–December 1997.

3 For original quotation see Susan Ratcliffe (ed.), *Oxford Essential Quotations (4 ed.)*, Oxford University Press, published online, 2016.

4 Shawn Achor, Andrew Reece, Gabriella Rosen Kellerman and Alexi Robichaux, "9 Out of 10 People Are Willing to Earn Less Money to Do More-Meaningful Work", *Harvard Business Review*, 6 November 2018.

5 Joseph Folkman, "8 Ways To Ensure Your Vision Is Valued", *Forbes*, 22 April 2014.

6 John T. Perry, Gaylen N. Chandler and Gergana Markova, "Entrepreneurial Effectuation: A Review and Suggestions for Future Research", *Entrepreneurship Theory and Practice*, Volume 36, Issue 4, July 2012.

7 Jim Collins and Jerry I. Porras, *Built to Last: Successful Habits of Visionary Companies*, third edition, Harper Business, 1994.

8 See "Address to Joint Session of Congress May 25, 1961", jfklibrary.org, accessed 5 January 2022.

9 Jan Trott, "Man walks on the moon: 21 July 1969", *Guardian*, 19 July 2019.

10 David C. McClelland, *Human Motivation*, Cambridge University Press, 1988.

11 The term "powerful oversimplification", originally coined by Bruce Henderson, founder of the Boston Consulting Group (BCG), describes the matrixes and models the consulting firm created to help frame business problems for clients. See Lawrence Freedman, *Strategy: A History*, Oxford University Press, 2013.

12 Howard E. Gardner, *Leading Minds: An Anatomy of Leadership*, Basic Books, 1995.

13 Kendall Haven, *Story Smart: Using the Science of Story to Persuade, Influence, Inspire, and Teach*, Libraries Unlimited, 2014.

14 This comes from a presentation on "Positive Intelligence" by Bill Carmody.

15 Paul Hekkert, Clementine Thurgood and T.W. Allan Whitfield, "The mere exposure effect for consumer products as a consequence of existing familiarity and controlled exposure", *Acta Psychologica*, Volume 144, Issue 2, October 2013.

16 Edgar Dale, *Audio-Visual Methods in Teaching*, third edition, Holt, Rinehart & Winston, 1969.

17 See "McDonald's Mission and Vision Statement Analysis", mission-statement.com/mcdonalds

18 George L. Roth and Anthony J. DiBella, "Balancing Push and Pull Change", *Systemic Change Management*, Palgrave Macmillan, 2015.

19 See Alison Rose, "CEO Alison Rose Day 1 speech", NatWest Group, 1 November 2019, www.rbs.com/rbs/news/2019/12/ceo-alison-rose-day-1-speech.html.

20 See Amanda Blanc, "Amanda Blanc: 2020 was truly Aviva at our best", www.youtube.com/watch?v=bz4rljrJf0o, 21 Dec 2020.

21 Garth S. Jowett and Victoria J. O'Donnell, *Propaganda and Persuasion*, SAGE Publications, third edition, 1992.

22 See bombardier.com/en/who-we-are/our-history.

23 Chris Loh and Luke Bodell, "The Rise and Fall of Bombardier Aerospace", *Simple Flying*, 12 June 2020.

24 See "From War to Partner: Airbus and the CSeries", *Leeham News and Analysis*, 18 October 2017.

25 Frédéric Tomesco, "What went wrong at Bombardier? Everything", *Montreal Gazette*, 8 February 2020.

26 Peggy Hollinger, "Airbus vows to make Bombardier aircraft a success", *Financial Times*, 8 June 2018.

Chapter 6: The Discipline of Political Savvy

1 See Michael D. Watkins, "Government Games", *MIT Sloan Management Review*, Winter 2003 and Michael D. Watkins, "Winning the Influence Game: Corporate Diplomacy and Business Strategy", *Harvard Business Review*, 2003.

2 David A. Lax and James K. Sebenius coined these terms. See "Thinking Coalitionally: Party Arithmetic, Process Opportunism, and Strategic Sequencing", in H. Peyton Young (ed.), *Negotiation Analysis*, University of Michigan Press, 1991.

3 Kurt Lewin, a pioneer in the field of group dynamics, proposed a model of social change based on the idea of driving and restraining forces. One of Lewin's fundamental insights is that human collectives – including groups, organizations and nations – are social systems that exist in a state of tension between forces pressing for change and forces resisting change: "[The behaviour of a social system is] . . . the result of a multitude of forces. Some forces support each other, some oppose each other. Some are driving forces, others restraining forces. Like the velocity of a river, the actual conduct of a group depends upon the level . . . at which these conflicting forces reach an equilibrium." See Kurt Lewin, *Field Theory of Social Science: Selected Theoretical Papers*, Harper & Brothers, 1951.

4 See Leo Ross and Richard E. Nisbett, *The Person and the Situation: Perspectives of Social Psychology*, second edition, Pinter & Martin Ltd., 2011.

5 See David Krackhardt and Jeffrey R. Hanson, "Informal Networks: The Company Behind the Chart", *Harvard Business Review*, July–August 1993.

6 See Virgil Scudder, Ken Scudder and Irene B. Rosenfeld, *World Class Communication: How Great CEOs Win with the Public, Shareholders, Employees, and the Media*, first edition, Wiley, 2012.

7 Aristotle, *The Art of Rhetoric*, trans. Hugh Lawson-Tancred, Penguin Classics, 1991.

8 Robert B. Cialdini, *Influence: The Psychology of Persuasion*, William Morrow, 1984.

9 James Clear, "Why Facts Don't Change Our Minds", https://jamesclear.com/why-facts-dont-change-minds, accessed 18 May 2023.

10 Roger Fisher and William Ury with Bruce Patton, *Getting to Yes: Negotiating an Agreement Without Giving In*, Houghton Mifflin, 1991.

11 See James K. Sebenius, "Sequencing to Build Coalitions: With Whom Should I Talk First?" in *Wise Choices: Decisions, Games, and Negotiations*, ed. Richard J. Zeckhauser, Ralph L. Keeney and James K. Sebenius, Harvard Business School Press, 1996.

12 The term "action-forcing events" was coined by Michael Watkins in "Building Momentum in Negotiations: Time-related Costs and Action-forcing Events" *Negotiation Journal*, Volume 14, Issue 3, July 1998.

13 For more information on this exercise, see Trainers Toolbox, "Perceptual positions: powerful exercise to strengthen understanding and empathy", www.trainers-toolbox.com/perceptual-positions-powerful-exercise-to-strengthen-understanding-and-empathy/, accessed 18 May 2023.

Conclusion: Developing Your Strategic-thinking Ability

1 Some of this advice is adapted from Nina A. Bowman, "How to Demonstrate Your Strategic Thinking Skills", *Harvard Business Review*, 23 September 2019.

2 Dana Asby, "Why Early Intervention is Important: Neuroplasticity in Early Childhood", Center for Educational Improvement, edimprovement.org/post/why-early-intervention-is-important-neuroplasticity-in-early-childhood, 9 July 2018.

ACKNOWLEDGEMENTS

This book results from a productive collaboration with Sebastian Murray, a gifted researcher, writer, and editor. Seb contributed substantially by doing background research, drafting several chapters' initial versions, and editing the manuscript. I very much appreciate his insight and support throughout the writing process.

Lucy Oates, my editor from Penguin Random House UK, commissioned this work. She saw an opportunity in the business book market for a serious but accessible treatment of strategic thinking. I was gratified when she reached out to me to see if I would take on the project. I also very much appreciate the support that her successor, Géraldine Collard, and her team gave me throughout the writing and editing process.

Thanks, too, to Hollis Heimbouch, Publisher at Harper-Business. Hollis saw the potential and committed herself and her team to supporting the book in North America.

The introduction to the book and many examples of strategic thinking in subsequent chapters tell the story of Gene Woods and his journey to become the CEO of Advocate Health, one of the largest non-profit healthcare systems in the United States. I have worked with Gene for over seven years and feel privileged to have supported him. He is one the greatest strategic thinkers I have known, as well as being a world-class CEO. I very much appreciate his willingness to let me share his story.

The research for the book included interviews with more than 50 executives, and their insights and quotations are featured throughout. I very much appreciate their willingness to share their experience. Special thanks to Camilo Cobos, Vice President of the Pharmaceutical Services Group at Thermo Fisher Scientific, for the substantial time he devoted to exploring the topic of strategic thinking with me.

My interest in strategic thinking was catalyzed over 30 years ago while earning my PhD in Decision Sciences at Harvard University and Harvard Business School. One of my thesis advisors was Howard Raiffa, an eminent developer of key concepts in game theory, decision theory, and negotiation theory. He sparked my interest in "games and decisions" and taught me strategic thinking frameworks and tools I have drawn upon throughout my career and in Chapter 3 on The Discipline of Mental Agility.

I feel fortunate to have wonderful colleagues whose work has contributed substantially to thinking about strategic thinking. I want to acknowledge especially the contributions of Amit Mukherjee and Albrecht Enders. The second half of Chapter 2 on The Discipline of Systems Analysis is based on work Amit and I did on designing adaptive organizations and what we called "The Four Wheel Drive Model." Elsewhere in the book, I mention important ideas Amit developed in his highly recommended books *The Spiders' Strategy* and *Leading in a Digital World*.

Chapter 4 on the Discipline of Structured Problem-solving was inspired and informed by the research and practice of

Albrecht Enders and our IMD colleague Arnauld Chevallier in their excellent book Solvable. Albrecht and I co-direct the Transition to Business Leadership Program at IMD, and I couldn't hope for a better colleague and friend. Watching Albrecht teach about the power of structured problem-solving to help leaders solve complex organizational problems convinced me that it was a crucial element of strategic thinking. Also, his hero-quest-treasure-dragon metaphor is a memorable and valuable way to organize the process.

The International Institute for Management Development (IMD) provided research funding that made it possible to research and write the book. I am grateful to the research support staff there, especially Cédric Vaucher, for their help in securing the needed resources. Many thanks as well to IMD President Jean-Francois Manzoni and Dean of Research Anand Narasimhan for their support and encouragement.

I very much appreciate the support of Rich Wetzler and the team at my consulting company, Genesis Advisers, for their patience and encouragement throughout the multi-year research and writing process.

The book is dedicated to my wife, Katia Vlachos. Katia encouraged me to take on this project when I was first offered it. I had doubts about embarking on something new, and she helped me see that I could and should. She also was a steadfast supporter as I sometimes struggled throughout the process. Without her support, this book would have never been written, and I greatly appreciate her.

INDEX

Note: page numbers in **bold** refer to illustrations, page numbers in *italics* refer to information contained in tables.

"7-S Framework" 43

Aaron, Marjorie 125, 126, 128
achievement 110
Ackman, Bill 42
acquisitions 21
action learning 156
action-forcing events 141
active listening 112, 117, 134, *135*, 142
advice-seeking 154
Advocate Aurora Health 3
Advocate Health 3
affiliation needs 110
agency 25
agendas 127, 128–9
Airbus 119
algorithms 38
alliances 108, 128–9, 140
AlphaGo (game) 23
alternative choices 131
ambiguity 9, 11, 84–5, 95, 128
    see also CUVA (complexity, uncertainty, volatility and ambiguity)
ambition 14, 109, 128
analysis
    case study 33
    competitive 11–12
    see also systems analysis

analytical skills 12, 13
analytics 157
Anyline 40
Approve, Support, Consult and Inform (ASCI) framework 89–91, *90*
architect's exercise 119–20
"architectural" models 39
Aristotle 136
Armstrong, Scott 78–9
artificial intelligence (AI) x, 16–17, 23, 38, 157
ASCI (Approve, Support, Consult and Inform) framework 89–91, *90*
"associative activation" 25
assumptions 7, 28, 57–9
Atrium Health 9, 21, 89, 95, 112–13, 115
    see also Carolinas HealthCare System
attention 27, 31, 42
autonomous vehicles 39, 47
Aviva 118

backward induction 73, 74
Bart, Chris 107
Beaudoin, Laurent 118–19
beliefs, consistent 138
Bellemare, Alain 119

Bennis, Warren G. 9
best practice 2, 30
biases, cognitive 24, 28–30, 93–4
Big, Hairy, Audacious Goals
        (BHAGs) 109
big picture 58–9, 148, 152
blaming others 29
Blanc, Amanda 118
body language 126–7, 141
Boeing 118
Bombardier 118–19
bottom-up approaches 112
boundaries 59
brain
    balancing the two halves of the 87
    exercising 147, 149–50
    left/right 87
    and pattern recognition 24, 31
    and priming 26
bridge 76
"bullseye" diagrams 132–3, **133**

Cairns, George 77–8
capabilities **43**, 44
carbon dioxide emissions 50
card games, competitive 76
Carolinas HealthCare System
        (CHS) 1–3, 20–1, 87–8
    see also Atrium Health
case study analysis 33
causal loop diagrams 59
cause-and-effect relationships 19,
        28, 37
    simple linear 58
Chabris, Christopher 27
challenges
    constructive 149
    and CUVA 9–11
    developing strategic thinking
        through 14
    and mental agility 65
    and pattern recognition 19–20,
        57
    recognising, prioritizing and
        responding to ix, 1–2, 4,
        7, 15, 19–20, 38, 57
    and System 2 thinking 25

and systems analysis 38, 57
    wide ranging solutions to 29
change 7, 10
    resistance to 48, 50
    see also volatility
chess 22, 68, 73, 76
Chevallier, Arnaud 92, 93
Chief Executive Officers (CEOs)
        1–4
    and mental agility 65–6, 74
    and pattern recognition 20–1,
        23–4, 25, 29, 33
    and structured problem-solving
        87–8
    and visioning 108–9, 118–19
choice 25
    alternative 131
choice-shaping 139
CHS see Carolinas HealthCare
        System
Cialdini, Robert B. 138
Clear, James 138
climate change 49–50
climate scientists 38
coalitions 128
cognitive biases 24, 28–30, 93–4
cognitive load 38
collaboration 12, 156
Collins, Jim 109
commitments, prior 138–9
communication, effective 12
competitive advantage 85, 157
competitive analysis 11–12
competitors 67, 69–70, 71–3
complexity 9–10, 11, 157
    and pattern recognition 21–2,
        27–8
    and structured problem-solving
        83–4, 89
    and systems analysis 38–9, 42,
        59–60, 151
    see also CUVA (complexity,
        uncertainty, volatility and
        ambiguity)
computer-based modelling 38–9
concentration 25
Cone of Experience model 115

confirmation bias 28–9
consolidation 68, 88
consultation 134, *135*
context 8, 16–17, 148
contingency 41
contracts, insecure 131
cooperation 67
COVID-19 pandemic 41–2
  vaccinations 41, 50
creativity 6–7, 12–13, 17, 157
  definition 7
  and structured problem-solving
    87, 93, 95
  versus strategic thinking 7
  Wallas' five-stage model for
    unleashing 97–8
crises
  economic 41
  prevention 55–7, **55–6**
crisis-management
  and learning from crises 53–5,
    53–4, 56, 57
  and systems analysis 53, 56, 57
critical thinking 6–7, 30, 85, 148
Cross, Nigel 7–8
Culleton, Paul 111, 115–16
curiosity, cultivation 32, 150
currencies for exchange,
    organizational 129–30, **130**
customer-centric organizations 45
customers
  awareness of the expectations and
    needs of 8
  creating solutions for 7–8
CUVA (complexity, uncertainty,
    volatility and ambiguity)
    9–11, 157
  and pattern recognition 15, 19,
    150
  and structured problem-solving
    83–5
  and vision 107

Dale, Edgar 115
data 157
data processing x, 16
De Havilland 118

decision-makers, understanding key
    129–31, **130**, *132*
decision-making
  and artificial intelligence 16
  biases in 93–4
  and entanglement 140
  in the face of uncertainty and
    change 7
  organizational **43**, 44
  and pattern recognition 24, 26
decisions, prior 138
deduction 12
Deep Blue 22
deep-learning 22–3
design thinking 7–8
development opportunities 156
devil's advocacy 78
Dewey, John 85
dialectical inquiry 78
diminishing returns 49
"double down" 29
Dow Chemical 65
"drive to win" 14

economic crises 41
economies of scale 2
"effectuation" 109
Eiklid, Rolf 127, 136
Einstein, Albert 91
Eisenberg, Harald 125–6, 128,
    130–1
electric vehicles 70–1
emotional intelligence 12–13, 17,
    141–3
employees, awareness of the
    expectations and needs of 8
encouragement *135*
end-users, creating solutions for 7–8
Enders, Albrecht 92, 93
Endowment element 12–13, 75,
    147
entanglement 139–40
equilibrium 47
  stable 69–70
era planning 73–4
ethos 136, *137*
evaluative criteria 94–5, **94**

evaluative skills 154
Ever Given (container ship) 40, 41
evocative descriptors 116
evolutionary biology 27
Exercise element 13, 14, 75, 147
experience
  learning from 19, 53–7, **53–4**
  openness to new 14
  and strategic thinking 13–14
Experience element 13–14, 75,
      147, 148–9
experts
  in pattern recognition 32, 150
  seeking advice/feedback from 154
exposure effect 115
external environment 8, 124, 148,
      157

"fast followers" 69
Federal Trade Commission 3
FedEx 33
feedback 34, 154
feedback loops 47–8
"fidelity of the model" 57–8
financial news media 28
first-mover advantage 68–9, 70–1
Fisher, Roger 139
Five Forces 12
flexibility 110
focus 27, 42
framing 134, 136–7, *137*, 139, 144
future-orientation 6–8, 14–15,
      75–6, 148

gains 93–4
Galbraith, Jay 43–4, **43**
"game trees" 71–3, **72**
game-playing 63–4, 66–7, 76, 79,
      152
game-theory, application 67–75
"garbage in, garbage out" 30
Gardner, Howard 114
General Electric (GE) 23–4, 134
global warming 49–50
Go (game) 22–3
goals 6, 109
Goldratt, Eliyahu M. 46

Google, DeepMind 23
government regulations 10
growth 3, 8, 37

halo effect 28–9
Haven, Kendall 114
healthcare 9–11
  consolidation 1–4, 20–1
  and structured problem-solving
      87–8, 95
  and vision 112–13, 115
  see also Atrium Health; Carolinas
      HealthCare System
"Hero's Journey" 92–3, 95
holistic approaches 38, 42

IBM 22
ideas
  new 7, 12
  "priming" 25
Immelt, Jeff 134
immersion 31–2, 34–5, 150
Inc. (business magazine) 33
inductive thinking 12
Infeld, Leopold 91
influence 16, 129, 154
  crafting strategies of 133–41, 144
  mapping networks of 132–3, **133**
  and sequencing 140–1
information overload 24
information processing 24, 30, 33
innovation 8, 157
intellectual inquiry, phases of 85
intelligence, emotional 12–13, 17,
      141–3
interconnectivity 157
international trade, vulnerabilities of
      40–1
investors 41–2
"Invisible Gorilla, The" 27

Jie, Ke 23
Johnson & Johnson 107, 111, 113
"just in time" production 40

Kahneman, Daniel 24–5, 26, 28
Kalin, Katherine Bach 42

Kasparov, Garry 22
Kelley, David 7
Kelley, Tom 7
Kennedy, John F. 109–10
Kinigadner, Lukas 40

Learjet 118
learning
    action 156
    from experience 53–7, **53–4**
level-shifting 63–6, 75–6, 79, 152
leverage points 45–6
limiting factors 46–7, 59
listening, active 112, 117, 134, *135*, 142
lockdown 41–2
logos 136, *137*
loss 93–4
    aversion to 93–4

machine learning systems 16
Management Research Group 4
Mandela, Nelson 108
marathon runners 13
market share 69–70, 72
McClelland, David 110
McDonald's 116
McKinsey 43
measures **43**, 44
memory 23–5
mental agility 15, 60, 63–80, 82
    checklist 79–80
    development 75–9, 149, 151–2
    and game-playing 63–4, 66–7, 76, 79, 152
    and game-theory application 67–75
    and level-shifting 63–6, 75–6, 79, 152
mental models 19, 151
    and immersion 31
    of organizations 10
    and pattern recognition 23–4, 30, 33–4
    problems with 30–1
    and systems analysis 37, 39, 59
mentors 154

mergers 21
metaphors 114
methane 50
mind, machine metaphor 28
mission 105–6, 108, 113
mission statements 107, 113
mobilization 15–16, 19, **81**, 82, 85, 155, **155**
    see also political savvy; structured problem-solving; visioning
models 37, 38, 60
    see also system models
motivational drivers 110–11, **111**
Mukherjee, Amit S. 51

Nanus, Burt 9
"narrative trap" 28
NatWest Group 118
Navicent Health 21
needs 8, 110, **130**
Neilley, Brad 113
network strategy 2
network-building 144, 148
neural networks 22
neuroplasticity 31, 149
non-linearities 48–50, 58
norms, social 138
novelty 83
Nowak, Alina 125–32, **133**, 136, 140

objectives 127, 129
    core (priorities) 105, 106, 110, 113
obligations 138
opportunities 6
    capitalizing on 83
    and developing experience 13–14
    development 156
    for growth 8, 37
    recognition/detection/ prioritization 15, **20**
        and mental agility 64, 65, 76
        and pattern recognition 19–21, 26–8, 30, 57, 150
        and systems analysis 37–8, 50–1, 57

opportunities – *Cont.*
　and the recognize-prioritize-
　　mobilize cycle **81**, 82,
　　155
　and structured problem-solving
　　82, 83
　and vision 114
opportunity cost 101
organizational culture **43**, 44–6, 48
　of strategic thinking 156
organizational currencies for
　　exchange 129–30, **130**
organizational design 43–4, **43**
　adaptive 50–1, 55–6
organizational performance 29
organizational structure **43**, 44
organizations, customer-centric 45

Parker, Michael 65–6
partnering models 2–3
pathos 136, *137*
pattern recognition x, 15–16,
　　19–35, 57, 63, 81–2
　checklist 35
　definition 19, 150
　development 24, 31–4, 149–50,
　　156
　how it works 23–6, 150
　limitations of 26–31
　and mental agility 68
　and systems analysis 38
　value of 21–3
　and vision 120
people **43**, 44
　reading 141–2
"perceptual position" exercise
　　142–3, **142**
performance, organizational 29
permafrost 50
Pershing Square Capital
　　Management 42
personality 14
perspective-taking 142–3, **142**,
　　149, 152
Pfizer-BioNTech COVID-19
　　injection 50
planning, strategic 12

point of view 148
Polar ice, melting of 49
political savvy 16, 17, 82, 123–45
　checklist 144–5
　developing 143–4, 149, 153–4
　and emotional intelligence 141–3
　and influence 129, 132–41, **133**,
　　144
　and understanding and embracing
　　politics 125–9
　and understanding key decision-
　　makers 129–31, **130**, *132*
Porras, Jerry I. 109
Porter, Michael 11–12
power dynamics 154
"power of fair process" 91, 124
power needs 110
"powerful simplification" 105,
　　113–18
prediction-making x
　and artificial intelligence 16
　and complexity 10
　and pattern recognition 19, 23–4
　and role-playing 78–9
　and systems analysis 15
　and uncertainty 10
present, being *135*
price wars 70
pricing strategies 69–70, 71–3, **72**
"priming" 25–6
prioritization 15, 19, 85
　of challenges ix, 1–2, 4, 7, 15,
　　19–20, 38, 57
　recognize-prioritize 81–2
　recognize-prioritize-mobilize
　　cycle **81**, 82, 155, **155**
　see also opportunities,
　　recognition/detection/
　　prioritization
probability 72–3, **72**, 84, 101
problem framing (problem
　　formulation/finding) 83,
　　85–8, **87**, *90*, 91–5, 101
problem-prevention subsystems
　　55–7, **55**–6
problem-solving 7
　and artificial intelligence 16

see also structured
    problem-solving
problems 20, **20**, 82–5
    "wicked big" 83–5
processes **43**, 44, 50–1
product development 39
project management 47
"pull" approaches 117, 124
purpose 106–7, 108, 110
"push" approaches 117

questioning *135*

"reading the room" 141–2
reciprocity 138
recognize-prioritize 81–2
    see also mental agility; pattern
        recognition; systems
        analysis
recognize-prioritize-mobilize
    (RPM) cycle **81**, 82, 155,
    155
reflective thinking 154
reframing 149
regulations 10
regulators 8
relationships 128–9
    human-artificial intelligence x,
        16, 23, 38
repetition 115, 136–7
reputation 138
"restraining forces" 48
retention rates 115
rewards **43**, 44
risks x, 6, 26
Roberto, Michael A. 96
role playing 78
root-cause analysis 96–7, **97**
Rose, Alison 118
Rosenzweig, Phil 29
"rules of the game" 124

scapegoats 29
scenario-planning 76–8, 120
Schmidt, Helman 107
"science of strategy, the" 66
scoring systems 98–101, *100*

selective attention 27–8
self-awareness 142
"self-serving bias" 29
Senge, Peter M. 46, 106–7
sequencing 71, 140–1
shareholders 8
signalling 69–71, 76
Simons, Daniel 27
simulations 34
situational pressures 130–1
Skogsbergh, Jim 3
Smith, Fred W. 33
social norms 138
social pressure 137–9
South Africa 108
stable equilibrium 69–70
stakeholders 71, 157
    and ambiguity 11
    anticipating the actions and
        reactions of 15
    and the ASCI framework 89–91,
        90
    awareness of the expectations and
        needs of 8
    building alliances with key 16
    involving 89–91
    and political savvy 123, 126, 144,
        154
    and role-playing 79
    and scenario-planning 77
    and structured problem-solving
        84–5, 89–92, *90*, 95, 103
    and vision 111, 112, 118
Star Model 43–4, **43**
state 47
status quo 7, 131
STC *see* strategic thinking capacity
stopping rules 96
stories 114–15
strategic approaches 93
strategic direction **43**, 44
"strategic perspective" 4
strategic planning 12
strategic thinkers 12–14
strategic thinking ix–xi
    and artificial intelligence 16–17
    and contextual awareness 8

strategic thinking – *Cont.*
  culture of 156
  definition 5–6, 149
  and design thinking 7–8
  developing your ability 147–57
  Endowment element 12–13, 75,
    147
  essential nature ix
  Exercise element 13, 14, 75, 147
  Experience element 13–14, 75,
    147, 148–9
  as fast lane to the top 4
  future of 156–7
  and mental agility 15, 60, 63–80,
    82, 149, 151–2
  and pattern recognition x,
    15–16, 19–35, 38, 57, 63,
    68, 81–2, 120, 149–50,
    156
  and personality 14
  and political savvy 16, 17, 82,
    123–45, 149, 153–4
  power of 1–17
  and the recognize, prioritize and
    mobilize cycle 20, **20**
  and structured problem-solving
    15, 79, 81–104, 149,
    152–3
  and systems analysis 15, 35,
    37–61, 63, 75, 81–2, 120,
    149, 151
  value 9–11
  versus creative thinking 7
  versus critical thinking 6–7
  and visioning 15, 82, 105–21,
    149, 153
  what it is not 11–12
strategic thinking capacity (STC)
    13–14, 147
strategic thinking teams, building
    154–6
strategy
  and artificial intelligence 16
  development 16, 26
  and influence 133–41, 144
  and pattern recognition 26
  science of 66

  and vision 105, 106, 113, 115,
    116
strategy games 22–3
structured problem-solving 15, 79,
    81–104
  checklist 103–4
  and decision-making 82–3
  development 103, 149, 152–3
  five-phase cycle of 85–103, **87**,
    90, **102**
    commit to a course of action
      86, **87**, *90*, 101–2
    deciding on the best option 86,
      87, *90*, 98–101
    defining roles and
      communicating the
      process 86, **87**, 89–91, *90*
    exploring solutions 86, **87**, *90*,
      95–8
    problem framing 85–8, **87**, *90*,
      91–5, 101
  leading processes 85–102
  and problems 82–5
Suez Canal 40, 41
summarizing *135*
sunk cost fallacy (wishful thinking)
    29
survival 27
symbiotic relationships, human-
    artificial intelligence x, 16,
    23, 38
synthesis 12
System 1 thinking 24, 26
System 2 thinking 24, 26
system models 42–6, **43**, 60, 96
  elements 42
  fidelity of 57–8
  interconnections/interfaces 42
  limitations of 57–8
  and problem-solving 84
  purpose/function 42
systems **43**, 44
  boundary definition 59
  stability 47–8
systems analysis 15, 35, 37–61, 63,
    75, 81–2
  checklist 61

definition 38–9
and designing adaptive
    organizations 50–1
development 58–60, 149, 151
and feedback loops 47–8
how it works 42–5
and learning from experience
    53–5, **53–4**
and leverage points 45–6
limitations of 57–8, 59
and limiting factors 46–7
and non-linearities 48–50, 58
and preventing future problems
    55–7, **55–6**
process 37
and responding to crises 53
and threat detection 50–2, **52**
and tipping points 48–50, 58
value of 39–43
and vision 120

Taleb, Nassim Nicholas 28
Tattle, Peter 113
Taylor, Troy 107
teams, strategic thinking 154–6
"theory of constraints" 46
thinking
    "systems" of 24–6
    see also strategic thinking
threat recognition/perception 15,
    20
and mental agility 64, 73, 76
and pattern recognition 19–20,
    21, 27, 28, 30, 150
and the recognize-prioritize-
    mobilize cycle **81**, 82,
    155
and structured problem-solving
    82, 83
and systems analysis 50–2, **52**,
    53–4, **53**, 55–7
threat-detection subsystem 51–2,
    52, 53–4, **53**
threats
    neutralizing 19–20, 83
    and vision 114
time demands 27

tipping points 48–50, 58
top-down approaches 2–3, 112
trade-offs 98, 100
trends 7, 32, 34, 148

uncertainty 7, 9, 10, 11, 77–8
and pattern recognition 24
and scoring systems 101
and structured problem-solving
    84, 101
    see also CUVA (complexity,
        uncertainty, volatility and
        ambiguity)
US Army 9
    "after-action review" 55
    "Center for Army Lessons" 55

value capture 67, 69, 71
value creation 69, 71
    and game-playing 67
    and pattern recognition 20
    and structured problem-solving 83
values
    consistent 138
    core 110, 116
    expected 72–3
van de Oudeweetering, Arthur 22
Van Horn Foods 125–31, 132,
    133, 136, 140
vision 2, 6, 105–21
    definition 105–7
    from personal to shared 110–13
    over-reaching 118–19
    and political savvy 124
    and structured problem-solving
        95
vision boards 118
vision statements 112–13, 114, 116
visioning 15, 82, 105–21
    checklist 121
    developing 109–10, 119–20,
        149, 153
    from personal vision to shared
        vision 110–13
    importance of 107–9
    limitations of 118–19
    microvisioning 153

visioning – *Cont.*
   and "powerful simplification"
      105, 113–18
"visioning workshops" 120
vocabulary 149
volatility 9, 10, 11, 84
   see also CUVA (complexity,
      uncertainty, volatility and
      ambiguity)
VUCA (volatility, uncertainty,
      complexity, ambiguity) 9
   see also CUVA (complexity,
      uncertainty, volatility and
      ambiguity)

Wake Forest Baptist Health 3
Wallace, David 126, 128,
   140
Wallas, Graham 97–8
Welch, Jack 23–4, 42
"win, drive to" 14
Woods, Gene 1–4, 9, 20–1, 30, 33,
   64–6, 87–9, **94**, 95,
   112–13
Wright, George 77–8

"yesable propositions" 139

Zenger Folkman 4